THE UNFINISHED MIND

HOW TO THINK, ADAPT, AND THRIVE IN A CHAOTIC WORLD

By: Ahmed Yahya

Copyright © 2025 by Ahmed Yahya

All rights reserved.

No part of this book may be reproduced, stored in a retrieval system, or transmitted in any form or by any means — electronic, mechanical, photocopying, recording, or otherwise — without the prior written permission of the author, except in the case of brief quotations used in reviews or critical articles.

This book is intended for informational and motivational purposes only. It is not intended as a substitute for professional advice, whether medical, psychological, financial, or otherwise. Readers are advised to consult appropriate professionals before making any significant decisions.

The author has made every effort to ensure the accuracy and completeness of the information presented. The views and opinions expressed are those of the author and do not necessarily reflect any official policy or position.

Unless explicitly stated, any names, characters, places, or incidents mentioned are used in an illustrative manner. Any resemblance to actual persons, living or dead, or actual events is coincidental.

TABLE OF CONTENTS

About The Author 1

Introduction 2

Chapter 1: The Unfinished Mind: Why Your Thinking Is Your Biggest Advantage 4

Chapter 2: Mental Traps That Keep You Stuck And How To Break Them 14

Chapter 3: The 3-Second Rule: When To Trust Your Gut Vs. When To Pause 25

Chapter 4: Cognitive Flexibility: The Skill That Separates Smart Thinkers From Everyone Else 36

Chapter 5: The Mental Agility Framework: Five Thinking Habits That Will hange Your Life 47

Chapter 6: Thinking In The AI Age: What Machines Can't Replace 59

Chapter 7: How To Stay Ahead When The Rules Keep Changing 70

Chapter 8: Decision Making Under Pressure 81

Chapter 9: The 30-Day Mental Upgrade Plan 91

Chapter 10: The Unfinished Mindset: How To Keep Evolving For Life 102

Conclusion 114

Bibliography 117

ABOUT THE AUTHOR

Ahmed Yahya

Ahmed Yahya is a seasoned business leader, writer, and mindset strategist with over four decades of experience in corporate leadership, entrepreneurship, and personal development. Ahmed pursued his MBA at the University of Liverpool, where he honed his expertise in leadership, strategy, and business transformation. His rich life experiences across business, leadership, and personal growth give him a deep understanding of how to cultivate a success-driven mindset. Now, as a writer and thought leader, Ahmed shares his wisdom through books, articles, and coaching programs. His work blends real-world business acumen with deep insights into human psychology, resilience, and personal transformation. His mission is to empower individuals to unlock their full potential and guide them toward success in their personal and professional lives. Ahmed tells his mentees, "Your mindset is the blueprint of your destiny—design it with vision, strengthen it with resilience, and success will become your way of life." As Ahmed continues to inspire and empower others, his legacy of visionary leadership and unwavering dedication to personal growth remains a beacon of hope and possibility for all who seek to create a life of purpose and fulfillment.

INTRODUCTION

In 1975, an engineer named Steve Sasson walked into a meeting at Kodak headquarters, holding a device that would change the world. It was a clunky, shoebox-sized machine that could take photos without film—the world's first digital camera. The Kodak executives laughed it off.

"That's cute," they said, "but no one will ever want to look at their photos on a television screen."

Kodak, the company that had dominated photography for over a century, had just invented technology that would revolutionize how humans capture memories. Instead of embracing this breakthrough, they buried it. They couldn't see beyond their existing business model, couldn't imagine a world without film, and couldn't adapt their thinking to new possibilities.

By 2012, Kodak filed for bankruptcy. A company that once employed over 145,000 people and was worth billions became a cautionary tale of what happens when we refuse to evolve our thinking.

We live in an era of unprecedented change. Artificial intelligence is reshaping industries, automation is transforming jobs, and the skills that mattered yesterday might be obsolete tomorrow. Yet most of us still think the same way we did decades ago. We cling to outdated mental models, resist new ideas, and fall into thinking traps that keep us stuck in the past.

The most successful people aren't those who know the most—they're the ones who can think flexibly, adapt quickly, and make smart decisions in the face of uncertainty. They understand that in a world of constant change, the ability to evolve your thinking is more valuable than any specific knowledge or skill.

This book isn't about becoming smarter in the traditional sense. It's about developing mental agility—the ability to think clearly, adapt swiftly, and thrive in chaos. Through real-world examples, practical exercises, and evidence-based strategies, you'll learn how to upgrade your thinking for a world that never stops changing.

You'll discover why some people make consistently better decisions while others get stuck in mental loops. You'll learn how to spot thinking traps before they derail you, how to stay ahead when the rules keep changing, and how to maintain clarity under pressure. Most importantly, you'll develop a mindset that embraces change instead of resisting it.

Your mind is never finished, it's constantly evolving, adapting, and learning. The question is: Are you actively shaping that evolution, or letting circumstances shape it for you? Because in today's world, having an unfinished mind isn't a weakness—it's your greatest strength.

Welcome to the journey of mental agility. It's time to upgrade your thinking for a future that's already here.

CHAPTER 1

THE UNFINISHED MIND: WHY YOUR THINKING IS YOUR BIGGEST ADVANTAGE

When Steve Jobs was fired from Apple, he didn't see it as the end—he used it as a reset, proving that success isn't about what you know, but how fast you can think, adapt, and reinvent yourself in an ever-changing world. This principle of mental adaptability isn't just theory—it's the difference between thriving and becoming obsolete in today's rapidly evolving world. While traditional education focuses on accumulating knowledge, the real key to success is your ability to unlearn, relearn, and adapt your thinking as circumstances change.

Technology has transformed the way we work, communicate, and solve problems in just the last decade. Those who cling to outdated thinking patterns find themselves struggling to keep pace, while mentally agile individuals embrace change as an opportunity for growth. Your brain isn't a static computer—it's a dynamic system capable of rewiring itself based on new experiences and challenges.

In 1985, Steve Jobs faced what many would consider a career-ending setback. The company he had co-founded, Apple, had just fired him. At 30, he went from being the visionary behind the Macintosh to a CEO without a company, a leader without a team, and a genius without a plan. Many would have allowed that moment to define them. They would have believed they had peaked, that their best thinking was already behind them.

But Jobs didn't do that. Instead of clinging to the past, he adapted.

Rather than sulking over Apple's betrayal, Jobs used his failure as fuel. He started a new company, NeXT, where he reimagined computer software and pushed design innovation further. He also acquired a small animation studio called Pixar, which would later revolutionize storytelling with hits like Toy Story. Instead of seeing his exit from Apple as an ending, Jobs treated it as a reset.

A decade later, Apple—struggling without its visionary—brought Jobs back. But this wasn't the same Steve Jobs who had left years earlier. He had evolved. His thinking had sharpened, his vision had expanded, and his ability to adapt transformed Apple from a failing tech company into the most valuable brand in the world.

The lesson? Steve Jobs wasn't successful because he was a genius—he was successful because he was mentally agile. He knew how to unlearn, rethink, and reinvent himself when the world changed. Instead of holding onto old ideas, he trained himself to question assumptions, embrace uncertainty, and keep evolving.

That's the power of an unfinished mind.

Let's explore why mental adaptability matters more than raw intelligence, how to develop cognitive flexibility, and specific techniques for training your brain to think better, faster, and smarter. You'll learn why treating your mind as a work in progress—rather than a finished product—is the ultimate competitive advantage in an age of constant change.

The journey to mental agility starts with understanding that your greatest asset isn't what you currently know—it's your capacity to learn, adapt, and evolve. In this book, you'll discover practical strategies for developing this crucial skill, ensuring you stay relevant and effective no matter the change or challenges that come your way.

Most people believe intelligence is fixed, but it's not.

For decades, people believed intelligence was fixed at birth—a genetic lottery that determined your cognitive ceiling. This mindset led many to accept their perceived limitations, believing they couldn't get any wiser. But groundbreaking neuroscience research has shattered this myth, revealing that our brains are far more adaptable than we once thought.

The concept of neuroplasticity—the brain's ability to form new neural connections throughout life—proves that intelligence isn't static. Every time you learn something new, solve a problem, or challenge your thinking, your brain physically changes. New neural pathways form, existing connections strengthen, and your cognitive capabilities expand. This isn't just theory; it's a biological fact.

Consider Maria, a software developer who believed she'd reached her intellectual peak in her thirties. When her company shifted to AI-driven development, she initially panicked, thinking she was too old to learn such complex systems. But instead of giving up, she decided to test the limits of her adaptability. She started with small challenges, gradually increasing complexity. Within six months, she wasn't just keeping up—she was leading her team in implementing AI solutions.

What changed wasn't her innate intelligence, but her approach to learning. By embracing difficulty and viewing challenges as opportunities for growth, Maria rewired her brain. Each new concept she mastered created new neural pathways, making the next learning challenge more straightforward to tackle.

This principle is relevant beyond technical skills. Whether you're learning a new language, mastering a complex strategy, or developing creative problem-solving abilities, your brain adapts and grows stronger through deliberate practice and challenge. The key is understanding that struggle isn't a sign of limited intelligence—it's the process through which we become smarter.

Think of your brain like a muscle. Just as physical exercise builds strength and endurance, mental challenges build cognitive capacity. When you push against the boundaries of what you think you can learn or understand, you're not hitting a fixed limit—you're expanding it.

The implications of this understanding are profound. It means that no matter your age, background, or current capabilities, you can enhance your cognitive abilities. The question isn't whether you can get smarter, but how you choose to train your mind.

This shift in perspective—from seeing intelligence as fixed to viewing it as malleable—changes everything. It transforms obstacles from threats into opportunities for growth. It turns the stress of learning into the excitement of expansion. Most importantly, it puts you in control of your cognitive development.

The next time you face a challenging problem or complex concept, remember your struggle isn't evidence of your limitations—it's the sensation of your brain growing stronger. Every moment of confusion, every complex problem, every new understanding is reshaping your neural networks, making you smarter in ways that were once thought impossible.

The real superpower? Mental adaptability

In the 1990s, a young trader named Sarah worked at a prestigious Wall Street firm. She had graduated top of her class, memorized every market theory, and could recite financial formulas in her sleep. But when the dot-com bubble burst in 2000, her extensive knowledge couldn't save her portfolio. Meanwhile, her colleague David, who had average grades from a lesser-known school, thrived during the market chaos. The difference? David's superpower wasn't his knowledge—it was his ability to adapt his thinking in response to changing market conditions.

This scenario plays out repeatedly across industries and careers. Traditional intelligence—the kind measured by IQ tests and academic achievements—matters less than cognitive adaptability: the ability to shift your thinking, challenge your assumptions, and navigate uncertainty with confidence.

Cognitive adaptability isn't just about learning new information—it's about unlearning outdated patterns and reframing challenges in real-time. When faced with unexpected situations, the adaptable mind doesn't freeze or cling to familiar solutions. Instead, it pivots, explores alternatives, and finds opportunities where others see obstacles.

Over the last decade, technology has transformed the way people work. Professionals who relied solely on technical expertise found themselves struggling as automation and AI reshaped their industries. Those who thrived weren't necessarily the most skilled—they were the ones who could adapt their roles, learn new capabilities, and find ways to complement rather than compete with technology.

Mental adaptability manifests in three key ways:

- Pattern Recognition: Quickly identifying similarities between seemingly unrelated situations.
- Cognitive Flexibility: Willingly abandoning outdated approaches when they no longer serve.
- Strategic Improvisation: Creating novel solutions by combining existing knowledge in new ways.

Take Alex, a marketing director who spent fifteen years mastering traditional advertising. When social media emerged, many of his peers dismissed it as a passing trend. But Alex recognized that while the medium was new, the core principles of human psychology and storytelling remained constant. He adapted his expertise to the digital landscape, combining proven marketing wisdom with the latest technology. Within two years, he had built a thriving digital agency while his competitors struggled to remain relevant.

The good news? Mental adaptability isn't a fixed trait—it's a skill you can develop through deliberate practice. Each time you embrace a new challenge, question your assumptions, or approach a problem from multiple angles, you strengthen your ability to adapt.

Start small: When facing a challenge, resist the urge to apply your usual solution. Instead, ask yourself:

- What if my current approach isn't the best way?
- What could I learn from seemingly unrelated fields?
- How would someone with a completely different background tackle this?

Mental adaptability doesn't mean abandoning your expertise or constantly changing direction. Instead, it means holding your knowledge lightly enough to update it when evidence suggests better approaches. It's about maintaining a learning mindset while applying your experience effectively.

In today's rapidly evolving world, mental adaptability isn't just an advantage—it's a necessity for survival. Those who cultivate this skill find themselves not just surviving change, but thriving because of it. They turn disruption into opportunity, uncertainty into innovation, and challenges into stepping stones for growth.

Remember: Your greatest asset isn't what you know today—it's your ability to adapt what you know for tomorrow's challenges. In a world where change is accelerating, mental adaptability isn't just another skill—it's the foundation that makes all other skills valuable.

Key takeaway: Thinking is a skill you can train, just like a muscle

In 1995, a young chess player named Josh sat across from his coach, frustrated after another loss. "I'm just not naturally good at chess," he complained. His coach smiled and pulled out a brain scan showing neural pathways before and after intensive chess training. The difference was striking—the trained brain showed denser neural connections, like a muscle that had grown stronger through exercise.

This simple truth—that thinking is trainable—revolutionizes how we approach mental development. Just as you wouldn't expect to bench press 200 pounds without training, you can't expect optimal thinking without deliberate practice. Your brain physically changes with use, forming new neural pathways and strengthening existing ones through a process called neuroplasticity.

Consider Emma, a data analyst who struggled with complex problem-solving early in her career. Instead of accepting this as a fixed limitation, she treated her analytical thinking like a muscle that needed training. She started with simple logic puzzles, gradually increasing complexity. Each day, she pushed her mental limits slightly further, just as an athlete progressively increases weights. Within six months, she was solving problems that once seemed impossible, leading her team in developing innovative solutions.

The science behind mental training is clear: when you engage in focused thinking exercises, your brain produces more myelin, a substance that helps neural signals travel faster and more efficiently. This process mirrors how physical exercise builds muscle fiber, making movements stronger and more coordinated.

Here are three fundamental principles of mental training:

- Progressive Overload: Challenge your thinking with increasingly complex problems.
- Recovery and Reflection: Allow time to process and integrate new mental patterns.
- Consistent Practice: Regular engagement matters more than sporadic, intense efforts.

The key is understanding that mental fatigue during learning isn't a sign of limitation—it's evidence of growth. When you struggle with a new concept or feel mentally exhausted after solving problems, you're building stronger neural pathways.

Take Marcus, a public speaker who once froze during presentations. He began training his mind systematically: first mastering breathing techniques, then practicing with small groups, gradually working up to larger audiences. Each step built upon the last, strengthening his mental resilience just as a runner builds endurance through progressive training.

This approach transforms how we view learning and adaptation. Instead of seeing mental capabilities as fixed traits, we recognize them as trainable skills. Whether you're learning a new language, mastering complex analysis, or developing creative problem-solving abilities, the principle remains: deliberate practice creates measurable improvement.

The implications extend beyond individual skills. In today's rapidly changing world, the ability to train your thinking—to build mental strength, flexibility, and resilience—becomes increasingly valuable. Those who actively develop their cognitive capabilities find themselves better equipped to navigate complexity, solve novel problems, and adapt to new challenges.

Remember: Every time you push through mental resistance, question assumptions, or tackle complex problems, you're not just completing a task—you're building stronger neural pathways. Your brain is adapting, growing, and becoming more efficient at processing information and generating solutions.

The journey to stronger thinking starts with accepting that mental growth requires deliberate practice. Just as physical fitness demands consistent training, mental agility develops through regular, progressive challenges. The question isn't whether you can improve your thinking—it's how committed you are to training your mind. As we conclude this chapter, reflect on the central message: your mind's capacity for growth is both remarkable and scientifically proven. The stories we've explored—from Steve Jobs' transformation after leaving Apple to Maria's journey in mastering AI development—prove that mental agility isn't a gift bestowed at birth but a skill cultivated through deliberate practice.

As we move forward, remember that your mind remains unfinished by design. This isn't a weakness—it's your greatest strength. Every challenge you face, every new skill you develop, and every assumption you question contribute to your brain's ongoing evolution.

CHAPTER 2

MENTAL TRAPS THAT KEEP YOU STUCK AND HOW TO BREAK THEM

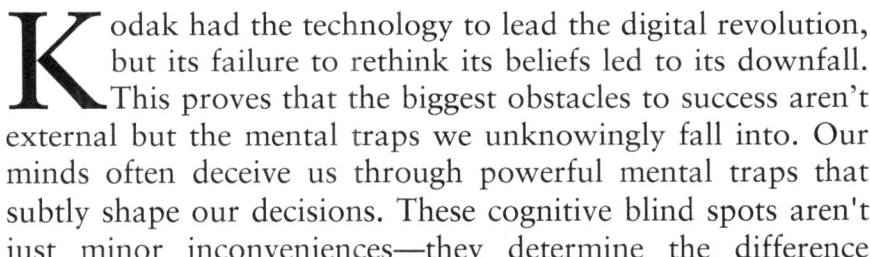

Kodak had the technology to lead the digital revolution, but its failure to rethink its beliefs led to its downfall. This proves that the biggest obstacles to success aren't external but the mental traps we unknowingly fall into. Our minds often deceive us through powerful mental traps that subtly shape our decisions. These cognitive blind spots aren't just minor inconveniences—they determine the difference between success and failure, innovation and stagnation, growth and decline.

The Kodak story illustrates one of the most dangerous mental traps: confirmation bias. The executives saw what they wanted to see, filtering out information that challenged their existing beliefs about the photography industry. They weren't stupid people—they were competent professionals caught in thinking patterns that made them resist change, even when change was essential for survival.

This resistance to new ideas isn't unique to Kodak. Every day, our brains default to comfortable patterns and familiar solutions, even when those patterns no longer serve us. We overthink simple decisions while making snap judgments about complex ones. We seek evidence that confirms our existing beliefs while dismissing information that challenges them. We cling to outdated strategies simply because they worked in the past.

But here's the truth: what trapped Kodak wasn't technology—it was thinking. The company had the resources, talent, and even the innovation to lead the digital revolution. What they lacked was the mental agility to break free from outdated beliefs and adapt to a changing world.

Here, we'll explore the most common mental traps that hold people back: fear-based decision making, cognitive biases, rigid thinking patterns, and the comfort of familiarity. Even more importantly, you'll master practical techniques to detect these traps in your thinking and develop the mental strength to overcome them.

Think of your mind like a sophisticated computer running on outdated software. The hardware might be powerful, but if the programming is flawed, the output will be too. By understanding and upgrading your mental software—your thinking patterns and decision-making processes—you can start processing information more effectively, making clearer decisions, and adapting faster to change.

The story continues with an engineer named Steve Sasson walking into that fateful meeting at Kodak headquarters. He held the future in his hands—the world's first digital camera. But the executives couldn't see it. Their mental traps had created invisible walls, limiting what they could imagine and accept. As we unpack this story and others like it, you'll begin to recognize similar patterns in your thinking and learn how to break free from them.

Here's what makes mental traps so dangerous: they don't feel like traps at all. They feel like wisdom, like common sense, like the right way to think. That's why the first step toward mental agility isn't learning new thinking patterns, it's understanding how your current patterns might be holding you back.

Why overthinking, biases, and old habits hold you back.

Picture your mind as a well-worn path through a forest. Each time you walk that path, it becomes deeper, more defined, and harder to deviate from. These are your mental habits—patterns of thinking that your brain has carved out through years of repetition. While these patterns can make daily decisions easier, they can also trap you in outdated ways of thinking.

Overthinking is like getting stuck in a loop on that path, circling the same trees without moving forward. Research in cognitive psychology shows that excessive analysis often leads to worse decisions, not better ones. When you overthink, you activate your brain's threat detection system, flooding your mind with cortisol and adrenaline. This stress response makes it harder to see opportunities, evaluate options clearly, or take decisive action.

Cognitive biases act like invisible guardrails along your mental path, subtly steering your thoughts in predetermined directions. Confirmation bias makes you notice evidence that supports your existing beliefs while filtering out contradicting information. Anchoring bias causes you to rely too heavily on the first piece of information you receive. Status quo bias makes you prefer things to stay the same, even when change would benefit you.

These biases served our ancestors well—they helped make quick decisions about danger and conserve mental energy. But in today's complex world, they can lead us astray. A financial advisor might miss investment opportunities because they conflict with their traditional strategies. A manager might overlook promising candidates because they don't fit the typical profile. An entrepreneur might stick with failing business models because it's what they know.

Old habits are particularly challenging because they operate below conscious awareness. They're like a default operating system running in the background of your mind. Breaking free requires more than just willpower—it demands conscious rewiring of neural pathways through consistent practice and exposure to new ways of thinking.

Consider Susan, a marketing executive who prided herself on thorough analysis. When tasked with launching a new product, she spent weeks gathering data, creating spreadsheets, and mapping out every possible scenario. While her colleagues moved forward with their projects, Susan remained stuck in analysis paralysis. By the time she felt ready to act, market conditions had changed, and the opportunity was lost.

The solution isn't to stop thinking—it's to think differently. Instead of trying to eliminate uncertainty through endless analysis, learn to act decisively with incomplete information. Rather than letting biases control your decisions unconsciously, bring them into awareness where you can examine and challenge them. Instead of clinging to old habits because they're comfortable, actively seek out new perspectives and approaches.

Mental agility requires regular maintenance, like clearing new paths through that forest of thoughts. Each time you challenge an assumption, question a bias, or try a new approach, you're creating alternative routes for your mind to travel. Over time, these new pathways become stronger, giving you more options for navigating challenges and opportunities.

The most successful people aren't those who think the most—they're the ones who think effectively. They've learned to recognize when overthinking is holding them back, when biases are clouding their judgment, and when old habits are keeping them stuck. Most importantly, they've developed the mental agility to break free from these traps when necessary.

Your brain will always try to conserve energy by falling back on familiar patterns. That's not a flaw—it's a feature of human cognition. The key is learning to recognize when these patterns serve you and when they limit you.

How your brain defaults to survival mode instead of growth mode.

Your brain has one primary directive: keep you alive. This survival-first mentality served our ancestors well when daily threats included predators and starvation. But in today's world, this ancient programming can work against us, keeping us trapped in patterns of defensive thinking when we need to grow and adapt.

When faced with uncertainty or change, your brain automatically shifts into survival mode. It releases stress hormones like cortisol and adrenaline, narrowing your focus to perceived threats while shutting down the neural pathways responsible for learning and innovation. This biological response made sense when encountering a saber-toothed tiger—you needed quick, defensive reactions, not creative problem-solving. But today, this same response can activate when facing a challenging work presentation or learning a new skill.

Jamila, a software developer, discovered that her company was transitioning to a new programming language. Instead of seeing an opportunity to expand her skills, her brain defaulted to survival mode. She felt threatened, anxious, and resistant to change. Her thoughts narrowed to protecting her current position rather than embracing the chance to grow. This defensive posture—focusing on what she might lose rather than what she could gain—is a classic example of the survival mindset at work.

The survival mode manifests in three common patterns. First, you prioritize avoiding losses over pursuing gains. Second, you gravitate toward familiar solutions even when they're no longer effective. Third, you resist new information that challenges your existing beliefs. These patterns create a self-reinforcing cycle: the more you operate from survival mode, the more you strengthen these defensive neural pathways.

But your brain also has an incredible capacity for growth. The key is learning to recognize when you're in survival mode and consciously shifting to what neuroscientists call the growth state. In this state, different neural networks activate, supporting creativity, learning, and strategic thinking. Your perspective broadens, allowing you to see opportunities where you previously only saw threats.

Take Carl, a small business owner whose sales plummeted during an economic downturn. His first instinct was to slash costs and cling to familiar strategies. But after recognizing this defensive pattern, he consciously shifted his thinking. Instead of asking, 'How do I survive this?' he asked, 'How could this challenge help my business evolve?' This mental shift led him to discover new market opportunities and innovative service models he wouldn't have considered in survival mode.

The brain's default to survival mode isn't a design flaw—it's a feature that needs updating. Like upgrading an operating system, you can train your brain to respond differently to challenges. This doesn't mean ignoring genuine threats or taking reckless risks. Instead, it means developing the ability to distinguish between actual dangers and opportunities for growth.

Start by paying attention to your physical and mental responses to change or uncertainty. Does your thinking become rigid? Do you feel an urge to retreat to familiar territory? These are signs that your brain has shifted into survival mode. When you notice these signals, pause. Take several deep breaths to activate your parasympathetic nervous system, which helps counteract the stress response. Then, consciously broaden your perspective by asking questions that promote growth-oriented thinking.

Remember, every time you override the survival response and choose growth, you're rewiring your brain. You're creating new neural pathways that make it easier to access growth mode in the future. This isn't about forcing yourself to be positive or ignoring legitimate concerns. It's about developing the mental agility to move between survival and growth modes as needed, rather than getting stuck in defensive patterns.

The most successful people aren't those who never experience survival mode—they're the ones who've learned to recognize it quickly and shift out of it intentionally. They understand that while survival thinking keeps you safe, growth thinking keeps you moving forward. In a world of constant change, the ability to make this shift is what separates those who thrive from those who fall behind.

Exercise: Identify 3 limiting beliefs that keep you from making smarter choices.

Now, it's time to turn inward and examine the invisible walls you've built in your mind. Take out a notebook or open a blank document. For the next ten minutes, you're going to identify three limiting beliefs that might be holding you back from clearer, sharper thinking.

First, reflect on moments when you hesitate to take action or make a decision. What thoughts ran through your mind? What stories did you tell yourself about why you couldn't or shouldn't move forward? Write down the first three that come to mind without censoring yourself.

Common limiting beliefs often fall into these categories:

- 'I'm not quick enough to make decisions under pressure'
- 'I need to have all the information before I can act'
- 'My way of thinking has worked so far, so why change it?'
- 'Smart people don't make mistakes'
- 'I'm too old/young to develop new thinking patterns'

Look at your list. Circle the three beliefs that appear most often in your thought patterns. These are your mental barriers—the invisible walls that keep you from making more intelligent choices.

Now, for each belief you've identified, answer these questions:

- Where did this belief come from?
- What evidence proves this belief is true?
- What opportunities have I missed because of this belief?
- How would my decisions be different without this belief?

Consider Rachel, a project manager who believed she needed to analyze every possible outcome before making decisions. This belief came from a past mistake where she made a quick choice that cost her team extra work. But when she examined this belief, she realized it had caused her to miss opportunities that required fast action. Her need for perfect analysis had become a bigger liability than the occasional quick decision.

The purpose of this exercise isn't to judge you or force immediate change. It's to bring awareness to the subtle ways your beliefs shape your choices. Think of these limiting beliefs like old software running in the background of your mind—they keep operating until you notice them and choose to update them.

For each limiting belief you've identified, write down a more flexible alternative:Instead of *I need all the information to decide,* try "I can make good decisions with incomplete information." Instead of *Smart people don't make mistakes,* try "Smart people learn from mistakes faster." Instead of *My thinking style works fine as is,* try "There's always room to sharpen my thinking."

Keep this list somewhere visible. Over the next week, notice when these limiting beliefs surface in your decision-making. Simply observing them in action will begin to loosen their grip on your choices. Remember, the goal isn't to eliminate these beliefs overnight, it's to recognize when they're controlling your decisions and gradually develop more agile thinking patterns.

Your mind is like a garden. Limiting beliefs are weeds that grow naturally but can choke out new growth if left unchecked. This exercise helps you identify those weeds so you can begin cultivating more productive thought patterns.

Mental traps aren't just inconveniences, they're invisible walls that shape our decisions, limit our potential, and often determine the difference between success and failure. The Kodak story serves as more than a cautionary tale; it demonstrates how even brilliant minds can become prisoners of their own thinking patterns.

Throughout this chapter, we've explored how overthinking paralyzes action, how biases distort judgment, and how the brain's default survival mode can prevent growth. These patterns don't just influence individual choices, they can collapse entire organizations, as we saw with Kodak's blindness to digital innovation.

But understanding these traps is only the first step. The real work begins with the conscious effort to recognize when we're caught in defensive thinking, stuck in analysis paralysis, or clinging to outdated beliefs. Mental agility isn't about avoiding these traps entirely—it's about developing the awareness to spot them and the flexibility to break free.

How have your thinking patterns held you back? Which decisions have you delayed because of overthinking? What opportunities have you missed because they didn't fit your existing beliefs? The exercise of identifying limiting beliefs isn't just an academic exercise, it's a practical tool for breaking free from mental patterns that no longer serve you.

As we move forward, remember that mental traps aren't permanent fixtures, they are habits that can be changed with awareness and practice. You can train your brain to shift from survival mode to growth mode, from rigid thinking to flexible adaptation, from fear-based decisions to strategic choices.

The executives at Kodak couldn't see beyond their mental walls. But you can. By understanding these traps and actively working to overcome them, you're already taking the first step toward greater mental agility.

CHAPTER 3.

THE 3-SECOND RULE: WHEN TO TRUST YOUR GUT VS. WHEN TO PAUSE

Some decisions must be made in an instant, while others require careful thought—but how do you know the difference? You're about to discover the 3-Second Rule — a simple yet powerful framework that helps you know when to trust your instincts and when to pause and evaluate. Using real-world examples like Captain Sully's heroic landing on the Hudson River, you'll learn how to make smarter, faster decisions under pressure. It will equip you to act confidently without falling into the trap of overthinking.

Understanding when to act swiftly versus when to step back and analyze is a critical skill that shapes our success in both life and work. This balance between intuition and deliberate thought isn't just about making better choices, but about training your mind to recognize which approach serves you best in any given situation.

The story of Captain Sully's Hudson River landing demonstrates this principle perfectly. It was January 15, 2009, and Captain Chesley "Sully" Sullenberger was about to make the most critical decision of his life. Minutes after takeoff from New York's LaGuardia Airport, US Airways Flight 1549 struck a flock of geese, causing both engines to fail. At 2,800 feet, the plane was losing altitude fast. In the cockpit, warning alarms blared, and passengers braced for the worst. Sully had seconds to decide what to do.

Air traffic control urged him to return to the airport. It was protocol. It was what the manual said to do. But Sully had flown for decades, trained his instincts, and knew the risks. In that moment, he didn't trust the standard playbook—he trusted his gut. Instead of turning back, he aimed for the Hudson River.

With only three seconds to act, Sully made a decision that went against conventional wisdom. And because of that, he saved the lives of all 155 people on board. When interviewed later, Sully explained: "I didn't have time to think in the traditional sense. I had to rely on my experience, my training, and my instincts."

This is the power of intuitive decision-making—when your gut instinct, sharpened by experience, can guide you faster than logic. But not every decision calls for split-second judgment. Sometimes, rushing to conclusions can lead to costly mistakes. The key is learning to distinguish between situations that demand immediate action and those that require deeper analysis.

By mastering the 3-Second Rule, you'll develop mental agility to shift between quick decisions and thoughtful analysis, ensuring you respond appropriately to every challenge you face. This isn't about choosing between gut feeling and logical thinking, iCt's about knowing when to use each, and how to leverage both for optimal results.

When intuition is your greatest tool vs. when it deceives you.

Your intuition is like a sophisticated pattern-recognition system built from years of experience. When a trader spots a market trend in milliseconds or a doctor diagnoses a rare condition at first glance, they're not just guessing—they're drawing on thousands of hours of pattern recognition stored in their subconscious mind.

But intuition isn't infallible. The same mental shortcuts that help us make rapid decisions can also lead us astray. Take Casey, a seasoned investment advisor with more than twenty years of experience helping clients navigate the markets. One morning, she felt an intense gut instinct about a certain stock — it reminded her of a big winner she had recommended years earlier. The patterns looked almost identical. Trusting that feeling, she encouraged several clients to invest heavily without thoroughly reviewing the company's financials. Six months later, the stock had lost 40% of its value. Her intuition, usually reliable, had been clouded by what psychologists call confirmation bias—seeing what we want to see based on past experiences.

The key is knowing when to trust your gut and when to pause for analysis. Your intuition works best in situations where you have extensive relevant experience and clear, rapid feedback. A firefighter who's tackling hundreds of blazes can instantly sense when a building is about to collapse. A chess grandmaster can spot a winning move in seconds. Their intuition has been calibrated through years of practice and immediate feedback.

However, your gut instinct becomes less reliable in unfamiliar territory or when dealing with complex, multi-layered problems. If you're facing a novel situation, venturing into a new field, or making decisions with long-term consequences, that's when you need to slow down and analyze.

Here's a practical framework to help you decide when to trust your intuition:

- You have deep experience in the specific domain.
- The situation requires immediate action.
- The patterns are clear and familiar.
- You've received accurate feedback on similar decisions.

Pause and analyze when:

- You're in unfamiliar territory
- The stakes are high and time permits
- Multiple factors are at play
- Your emotional state might cloud judgment

The power lies not in choosing between intuition and analysis, but in knowing when to use each. Think of them as different tools in your mental toolkit—each valuable in the right context.

Consider this: A seasoned emergency room doctor instantly recognizes a heart attack because they've seen thousands of cases. Their intuition, honed through experience, saves precious minutes. But when that same doctor faces a patient with unusual symptoms, they switch to methodical analysis—running tests, consulting colleagues, and carefully weighing options.

Training your intuition requires deliberate practice and honest feedback. Start by tracking your gut decisions and their outcomes. When your intuition proves right, identify the patterns that triggered it. When it leads you astray, analyze what you missed. Over time, you'll develop a refined sense of when to trust your instincts and when to dig deeper.

Remember, intuition isn't mystical, it's your brain processing patterns faster than your conscious mind can analyze them. By understanding its strengths and limitations, you can harness this powerful tool while guarding against its pitfalls. The goal isn't to always trust your gut or to always override it. It's to develop the wisdom to know the difference.

The "3-Second Rule" for making faster, better decisions

The 3-Second Rule isn't about rushing decisions, it's about training your mind to recognize when quick action serves you better than prolonged analysis. This mental framework, developed through studying high-performance decision-making, helps you navigate the critical space between impulse and paralysis.

Imagine you're driving and spot a red light ahead. You don't spend minutes analyzing whether to stop—you react within seconds based on learned patterns and clear signals. This same principle applies to many life decisions, where your initial assessment often contains the essential information needed to act.

Here's how the 3-Second Rule works:

- In the first second, your brain processes the immediate situation and available information.
- In the second, you assess the potential consequences of immediate action versus delay.
- In the third second, you make a clear choice: act now or step back for deeper analysis.

This framework isn't about making every decision in three seconds—it's about quickly determining which decisions need immediate action and which require more thought. A seasoned trader named Skyler demonstrates this principle daily. When market volatility spikes, he uses the first three seconds to decide whether to make an immediate trade or step back for detailed analysis. His success rate improved significantly after implementing this approach, not because he made every decision faster, but because he learned to distinguish between opportunities that required quick action and those that demanded deeper investigation.

This rule works best when you've built a foundation of knowledge and experience in your field. A novice trader attempting to make split-second decisions would likely fail—their intuition hasn't been calibrated through experience. The 3-Second Rule becomes powerful only after you've developed expertise in your domain.

To implement this approach effectively:

- Practice rapid pattern recognition in low-stakes situations.
- Build a mental database of scenarios through deliberate experience.
- Learn to recognize your emotional state during decision-making.
- Develop clear criteria for when to act quickly versus when to analyze.

During her first year, Anna, a new emergency room physician, struggled with the pressure of rapid decision-making. Every case seemed to require extensive analysis. But as she gained experience, she developed an intuitive understanding of which cases needed immediate intervention, and which could wait for more thorough examination. The 3-Second Rule became her framework for treating patients effectively—not by making snap judgments, but by quickly determining the appropriate decision-making pathway for each situation.

The beauty of this approach lies in its flexibility. It's not about forcing quick decisions but about developing mental agility to choose the right decision-making speed for each situation. Sometimes, those three seconds will tell you to stop and analyze. Other times, they'll confirm that immediate action is your best option.

Remember: The goal isn't speed for speed's sake, it's about developing the judgment to know when quick action serves you better than extended analysis. This skill becomes increasingly valuable in our fast-paced world, where opportunities and challenges often appear and disappear in moments.

By practicing the 3-Second Rule, you're not just learning to make faster decisions, you're training your mind to quickly determine the appropriate decision-making approach for any situation. This mental agility becomes a competitive advantage in both professional and personal contexts, allowing you to act decisively when needed while avoiding impulsive choices in situations that demand deeper thought.

Real-world example: How elite athletes and CEOs make decisions quickly under pressure.

When Michael Jordan faced the Utah Jazz in Game 5 of the 1997 NBA Finals, he was battling severe food poisoning. Despite his physical condition, he scored 38 points and made the game-winning shot. What allowed him to perform at such a high level wasn't just physical prowess—it was his trained ability to make split-second decisions under extreme pressure.

Elite athletes and successful CEOs share a common trait: they've developed specific mental frameworks that allow them to process information and make decisions rapidly under pressure. This isn't about natural talent, it's about deliberate practice and proven strategies that anyone can learn.

Let's examine how they do it:

- They simplify complex situations into essential elements.
- They maintain emotional control through practiced breathing techniques.
- They focus only on variables they can control.
- They trust their training and preparation.
- They embrace pressure as a performance enhancer.

In volatile markets, Lena Chen, a derivates trader has seconds to decide whether to execute trades that could result in massive gains or losses. Over years of experience, she's developed a mental checklist that she runs through in moments of high pressure: market context, risk parameters, and potential outcomes. This systematic approach allows her to make confident decisions in seconds rather than getting paralyzed by analysis.

The key difference between high performers and average decision-makers isn't that they think faster, it's that they've trained themselves to focus on the right information at the right time. They've learned to filter out noise and zero in on critical factors that influence outcomes.

This ability isn't magic, it's methodology. Elite performers practice decision-making under pressure regularly, often through simulation and scenario training. They deliberately expose themselves to high-pressure situations in controlled environments, allowing them to develop and refine their decision-making processes.

A fascinating example comes from the world of emergency medicine. Dr. James Thompson, a veteran ER physician, explains how experienced doctors make life-saving decisions in seconds: "We don't make faster decisions than novice doctors. We just know which information matters most. While a newer doctor might try to gather every possible data point, experience has taught us which signs tell the whole story."

This principle applies across fields. Whether you're an athlete, executive, or professional in any field, the key to making better decisions under pressure lies in:

- Building a robust mental framework through deliberate practice.
- Developing clear criteria for what information matters most.
- Training yourself to maintain focus under stress.
- Creating simple decision trees for common scenarios.
- Regular exposure to pressure situations in controlled environments.

The goal isn't to eliminate pressure—it's to harness it. Research in performance psychology shows that moderate levels of pressure can enhance decision-making when properly channeled. The key is developing systems that allow you to process information efficiently when stakes are high.

Remember: Quick decisions don't mean hasty ones. Elite performers make rapid choices not because they're rushing, but because they've trained themselves to recognize patterns and prioritize information effectively. Their speed comes from preparation and practice, not impulse.

By studying and applying these principles, you can develop the same mental agility that allows top performers to thrive under pressure. The key is consistent practice and a willingness to learn from both successes and failures. The power to make quick, effective decisions isn't just a gift, it's a skill you can develop through deliberate practice and understanding. As we've seen through Captain Sully's split-second choice to land on the Hudson River, the right decision at the right moment can change everything. But equally important is knowing when to step back and analyze, like Casey, the investment advisor, discovered when rushing into a familiar-looking trade.

The 3-Second Rule provides a practical framework for distinguishing between situations that demand immediate action and those that require deeper thought. This mental model isn't about making every decision in three seconds—it's about quickly determining which decisions need immediate action and which require more analysis.

Successful decision-making balances two crucial elements: the rapid pattern recognition that comes from experience, and the wisdom to know when those patterns might mislead us. Elite performers across fields—from emergency room doctors to traders—demonstrate that mental agility isn't about thinking faster but thinking better.

As you move forward, remember that improving your decision-making skills requires both practice and patience. Start with low-stakes decisions to build confidence in your judgment. Pay attention to the outcomes of your choices, learning from both successes and setbacks. Over time, you'll develop a refined sense of when to trust your instincts and when to pause for deeper analysis.

The key takeaway isn't that quick decisions are always better, or that careful analysis is always right. Instead, success lies in developing mental agility to recognize which approach serves you best in any given situation. This balance between intuition and analysis, between quick action and careful thought, is what separates effective decision-makers from those who either act too hastily or get paralyzed by analysis.

CHAPTER 4

COGNITIVE FLEXIBILITY: THE SKILL THAT SEPARATES SMART THINKERS FROM EVERYONE ELSE

Blockbuster had everything—money, market dominance, and millions of loyal customers—yet they failed because they couldn't see beyond their own outdated thinking. Meanwhile, Netflix adapted, evolved, and took over the industry. Let's discover why cognitive flexibility is the ultimate success skill, how rigid thinking silently destroys opportunities, and how you can train your brain to adapt faster, think smarter, and see possibilities before everyone else does.

In today's world, it's not the smartest who win—it's the most adaptable. The story of Blockbuster's demise isn't just about poor business decisions, it's a stark illustration of how rigid thinking can blind us to reality. When confronted with Netflix's innovative approach, Blockbuster's leadership couldn't break free from their established mental models. They were trapped by cognitive inflexibility, a psychological barrier that prevents us from adapting our thoughts and behaviors when circumstances change.

This same pattern repeats across industries, careers, and personal lives. People who excel aren't necessarily the most intelligent, they're the ones who can shift perspectives quickly, challenge their assumptions, and adapt their thinking to new situations. They possess cognitive flexibility, the mental ability to switch between different concepts, consider multiple aspects of an idea simultaneously, and adjust their behavior in response to changing environments.

In 2000, Reed Hastings, the CEO of a small DVD rental company called Netflix, walked into a meeting with Blockbuster's top executives. At the time, Blockbuster was an unstoppable giant—with over 9,000 stores and billions in revenue. Hastings had a simple offer:

"Buy Netflix for $50 million. Let's build the future of entertainment together."

The Blockbuster executives laughed him out of the room.

"People love renting movies in stores," they said. "No one wants to get DVDs in the mail, let alone stream them over the internet."

Their rigid thinking cost them everything.

Within a decade, Blockbuster was bankrupt, and Netflix was worth billions. Today, Netflix dominates the entertainment industry, while Blockbuster exists as nothing more than a cautionary tale of what happens when you refuse to adapt.

We will evaluate how mental rigidity silently undermines success, why some people adapt effortlessly while others struggle, and most importantly, how you can train your brain to become more cognitively flexible.

Think of cognitive flexibility as a mental muscle—one that grows stronger with deliberate practice. Just as athletes train their bodies to respond instantly to changing game conditions, you can train your mind to pivot smoothly between different perspectives, solutions, and strategies. This ability to shift mental gears quickly and effectively isn't just helpful, it's becoming essential for survival in an increasingly complex and unpredictable world.

As we move forward, you'll learn practical techniques to break free from rigid thinking patterns, exercises to strengthen your cognitive flexibility, and strategies used by adaptive thinkers to stay ahead of change.

Why rigid thinking kills opportunities and how to stay mentally flexible

Rigid thinking is a silent killer of potential, quietly destroying opportunities before we even recognize them. It's not just about being stubborn or set in our ways, iZt's about how our brains naturally resist change, even when that change could benefit us. This resistance stems from our brain's preference for familiar patterns and established neural pathways, making it easier to stick with what we know rather than explore new possibilities.

Zoe, a talented graphic designer spent fifteen years mastering Adobe Photoshop. When her industry began shifting toward digital UI/UX design, she dismissed the change. "I'm a print designer," she would say, "That's what I do." Her identity had become so intertwined with her existing skills that she couldn't see the bigger picture—that design was evolving, and she needed to evolve with it. By the time she realized her mistake, many of her colleagues had already adapted and advanced, while she struggled to catch up.

Rigid thinking manifests in three primary ways that kill opportunities:

- Status Quo Bias: Overvaluing the current state and resisting change even when the benefits are clear.
- Confirmation Bias: Seeking information that supports existing beliefs while ignoring contradictory evidence.
- Fixed Identity: Defining yourself by what you currently do rather than what you could become.

But mental flexibility can be developed through deliberate practice. Start by challenging your assumptions daily. When you catch yourself saying "That's just how it is" or "That's not how we do things," pause and ask, "Why not?"

This simple question opens doors to possibilities your rigid thinking might have blocked.

Develop the habit of considering multiple perspectives. When faced with a problem or decision, force yourself to generate at least three different solutions. Even if they seem impractical at first, this exercise trains your brain to move beyond its default patterns.

One powerful technique for building mental flexibility is the 'Reverse Assumption' method. Take something you believe is true about your work, life, or industry, and ask: "What if the opposite were true?" This isn't about proving yourself wrong, it's about expanding your mental horizons.

Mental flexibility also requires emotional awareness. Our strongest resistance to change often comes from fear or discomfort rather than logic. Learning to recognize when your emotional attachment to current methods, beliefs, or identities is preventing you from seeing new opportunities.

Practice regular mental resets by exposing yourself to new experiences, ideas, and challenges. Learn a skill completely different from your expertise. Read books from unfamiliar genres. Have conversations with people who hold opposing viewpoints. Each of these experiences creates new neural pathways, making your brain more adaptable.

Remember that mental flexibility isn't about abandoning your core values or expertise. It is about maintaining a learning mindset that allows you to adapt and grow. The goal isn't to change everything about how you think, but to develop the ability to shift perspectives when necessary.

To stay mentally flexible, practice the following:

- Question your initial reactions to new ideas.
- Seek out diverse perspectives and experiences.
- Embrace temporary discomfort as a sign of growth.
- View challenges as opportunities to expand your thinking.

The world rewards those who can adapt their thinking to changing circumstances. By developing mental flexibility, you're not just preparing for change—you're positioning yourself to recognize and seize opportunities that rigid thinkers can't even see. The key is to make mental flexibility a daily practice rather than waiting for circumstances to force you to adapt.

Mental flexibility is like muscle growth. It grows stronger with regular exercise but weakens with disuse. The more you practice viewing situations from different angles and challenging your assumptions, the more natural it becomes. Eventually, what once felt like mental gymnastics becomes your default way of thinking, allowing you to navigate change with confidence and spot opportunities others miss.

How to see problems from multiple angles and make smarter choices

Picture a detective examining a crime scene. They don't just look straight ahead—they crouch down, look up, walk the perimeter, and use different tools to uncover evidence. This same principle applies to problem-solving in everyday life. Viewing challenges from multiple angles isn't just helpful, it's essential for making better decisions.

When customer complaints about their app started rising, Ryan, a product manager's initial response was to blame the user interface. It seemed obvious that customers were struggling to navigate the app, so the design must be the problem. But Ryan remembered a valuable lesson from his mentor: "The first solution you see is rarely the best one."

Instead of jumping to conclusions, Ryan used a technique called The Five Perspectives Method. He examined the problem from different viewpoints:

- Technical: Was the app's performance causing issues?
- User Experience: How were people using the app?
- Business: Did the pricing model affect usage patterns?
- Market: What were competitors doing differently?
- Cultural: Were there regional differences in how people used the app?

This systematic approach revealed something unexpected—the real issue wasn't the interface, but rather how the app processed data in different time zones. A simple technical fix solved what initially appeared to be a design problem. By resisting the urge to accept the first obvious solution, Ryan saved his company months of unnecessary redesign work.

To develop this multi-angle thinking ability, start with these practical exercises:

- The Reversal Technique: When facing a problem, ask "What if the opposite were true?"
- Role Shifting: Consider how different stakeholders would view the situation.
- Time Frame Analysis: Examine the issue's past, present, and potential future impact.

Avery, a restaurant owner's initial instinct was to lower prices, when she was struggling with declining lunch sales, but she chose to apply the multi-angle thinking:

First, she gathered data from different perspectives:

- Customer feedback through surveys
- Employee observations about rush hour patterns
- Local business development plans
- Neighborhood demographic changes

This comprehensive analysis revealed the issue wasn't pricing—the neighborhood was shifting from office workers to remote employees. The solution? She transformed her lunch service into a hybrid model, adding delivery options and creating 'work-from-home' lunch packages.

The key to seeing problems from multiple angles lies in developing systematic thinking habits:

- Question Initial Assumptions: Your first interpretation is often limited by your immediate perspective.
- Seek Contrary Evidence: Actively look for information that challenges your current view.
- Consider Second-Order Effects: Think beyond immediate consequences to long-term impacts.

When examining any situation, use these guiding questions:
- What am I not seeing?
- Who else is affected by this?
- What would this look like in a different context?

Remember that multi-angle thinking isn't about making decisions more complicated, it's about making them more complete. By systematically exploring different perspectives, you reduce blind spots and increase the likelihood of finding optimal solutions.

This approach requires patience and practice. Start with small decisions and gradually apply these techniques to more complex challenges. The goal isn't to analyze every situation exhaustively but to develop the habit of looking beyond your initial perspective.

Over time, this multi-angle approach becomes second nature, leading to more nuanced understanding and better decision-making. It transforms how you approach challenges, turning what might seem like insurmountable problems into opportunities for innovative solutions.

The most valuable outcome of multi-angle thinking isn't just better solutions—it's developing a more comprehensive understanding of the challenges you face. This deeper insight often reveals opportunities that would have remained hidden from a single perspective.

Exercise: The "Perspective Shift Challenge," solving a problem using 3 different viewpoints

Now, it's time to put multi-angle thinking into practice with the Perspective Shift Challenge. This exercise trains your brain to automatically consider different viewpoints when facing any problem, leading to more innovative and comprehensive solutions.

Here's how it works:

- Choose a current challenge you're facing (personal or professional)
- Examine it from three distinct perspectives
- Document insights and potential solutions from each viewpoint
- Synthesize the findings into an action plan

Let's follow Jamie, a marketing manager, as she applies this technique to a real challenge: declining engagement on her company's social media channels.

Perspective 1: The Data Analyst From this viewpoint, Jamie examines metrics and patterns:

- Post engagement rates across different times
- Content categories that generate most interaction
- Demographic shifts in follower base
- Platform algorithm changes

Insights: Data shows the highest engagement during morning hours, with video content performing 3x better than static posts. The follower demographic has shifted younger over six months.

Perspective 2: The Customer

Jamie steps into her audience's shoes:

- What value do they seek?
- When and how do they consume content?
- What competing demands do they face? - What frustrations might they have?

Insights: Followers want practical tips they can apply immediately, prefer quick-format content, and engage more with authentic behind-the-scenes material than polished corporate posts.

Perspective 3: The Competitor Analyzing the market landscape:

- What successful strategies are others using?
- Where are gaps in current offerings?
- What unique angle could set her content apart?
- What mistakes should be avoided?

Insights: Competitors focus heavily on promotional content, leaving space for educational and community-building posts. Several successful accounts use employee spotlights effectively.

By synthesizing these perspectives, Jamie develops a comprehensive solution: restructuring content strategy to focus on morning posts, emphasizing video formats, showcasing team members, and creating educational series that deliver quick, actionable value.

Now, it's your turn. Choose a current challenge and apply the three perspectives:

The Analytical View
- Focus on facts, data, and measurable elements
- What do the numbers tell you?
- What patterns emerge?

The Human View
- Consider emotions, needs, and experiences
- How do people interact with this issue?
- What unstated needs exist?

The Strategic View
- Examine the broader context
- What long-term implications exist?
- Where are the opportunities?

CHAPTER 5

THE MENTAL AGILITY FRAMEWORK: FIVE THINKING HABITS THAT WILL CHANGE YOUR LIFE

Borders used to be one of the most powerful bookstore chains in the world, but when Amazon emerged, it ignored the shift, clung to old ways of thinking, and waited too long to adapt—until it was too late. Here, you'll discover how mental rigidity kills progress, why failing to adjust leads to failure, and how to train your brain to anticipate change instead of reacting to it. Through real-world lessons and The Mental Agility Framework, you'll learn how to think like a disruptor, stay ahead of the curve, and ensure that—no matter how the world evolves—you are always one step ahead.

The story of Borders serves as a stark reminder that success isn't just about size, resources, or market dominance, it's about developing the mental agility to recognize shifts, challenge assumptions, and adapt before it's too late. While Borders executives clung to outdated beliefs about consumer behavior, they missed the fundamental transformation happening in retail, reading habits, and technology.

The Mental Agility Framework is a practical system of five core thinking habits that distinguish those who thrive from those who get left behind. These aren't theoretical concepts, but battle-tested strategies used by innovators, entrepreneurs, and leaders who consistently stay ahead of change.

For years, Borders was one of the biggest bookstore chains in the world. With over 1,200 stores worldwide, it was a household name, packed with bestsellers, coffee shops, and loyal customers who loved the in-store experience.

Then, a new competitor emerged. Amazon.

At first, Borders didn't see Amazon as a threat. Online shopping was still new, and executives at Borders believed people would always prefer the in-store experience.

When Amazon started selling books online, Borders ignored it. When Amazon introduced one-click shopping, Borders doubled down on expanding physical stores. When Amazon launched the Kindle e-reader, Borders dismissed e-books as a fad.

Instead of building its own online bookstore, Borders outsourced its e-commerce operations to Amazon itself. Borders literally handed its future to its biggest competitor.

This isn't just a story about technological disruption—it's about the dangerous consequences of rigid thinking. The Mental Agility Framework you're about to learn will help you avoid these cognitive traps, giving you specific tools to sharpen your decision-making, challenge your assumptions, and build the mental flexibility needed to thrive in uncertainty.

By mastering these five thinking habits, you'll develop the cognitive agility to spot opportunities others miss, make smarter decisions under pressure, and continuously evolve your thinking as the world changes around you. Because in today's fast-moving environment, your success depends less on what you know and more on how quickly you can learn, unlearn, and adapt.

The five simple shifts that make your brain sharper every day.

Your brain is remarkably adaptable, capable of forming new neural connections and pathways throughout your life. This neuroplasticity means you can actively train your mind to become sharper, faster, and more agile through consistent practice and the right mental habits. Let's explore five fundamental shifts that can transform your cognitive capabilities.

The first shift is from passive consumption to active processing. Instead of mindlessly absorbing information, engage with it critically. When reading, pause regularly to summarize key points in your own words. Ask questions about the material. Consider how it connects to what you already know. This active engagement strengthens neural pathways and improves retention. A practical way to implement this is the 50/10 rule: For every 50 minutes of learning, spend 10 minutes processing and reflecting on what you've learned.

The second shift focuses on cross-pollination of ideas. The brain becomes sharper when you connect concepts across different domains. If you're in finance, study biology. If you're interested in technology, learn about architecture. These seemingly unrelated fields often reveal surprising patterns and insights that can enhance your problem-solving abilities. This cognitive cross-training builds mental flexibility and creates new neural connections.

The third shift involves embracing productive discomfort. When your brain encounters challenging tasks, it creates new neural pathways to adapt. Start your day with a complex problem before checking email. Learn a new skill that stretches your capabilities. The initial struggle is a sign of your brain building new connections and becoming stronger.

The fourth shift requires moving from multitasking to deep focus. Despite popular belief, multitasking weakens cognitive performance. Instead, practice single tasking with increasing duration. Start with 25 minutes of uninterrupted focus, gradually extending to longer periods. This builds mental endurance and improves processing power.

The fifth shift transforms how you handle mistakes. Rather than avoiding errors, see them as valuable feedback for your brain's learning process. When you make a mistake, your brain sparks new neural connections in its effort to correct and improve. Take time to analyze errors, understand their root causes, and adjust your approach.

Implementing these shifts requires consistency rather than intensity. Small, daily actions create lasting neural pathways more effectively than sporadic intense efforts. Start with one shift, practice it until it becomes natural, then add another. Your brain will respond by becoming progressively sharper, more adaptable, and better equipped to handle complex challenges.

Morgan, a software developer, started each morning by dedicating 10 minutes to intentionally reflect on and absorb what she had learned the day before. She practiced this shift for six months. She would read books about psychology and design, connecting these insights to her coding work. She tackled complex programming problems first thing each morning when her mind was fresh. She blocked out two hours daily for deep, uninterrupted coding sessions. Most importantly, she started keeping a 'bug journal' to analyze and learn from her coding mistakes.

The results were transformative. Her code became more elegant and efficient. She found creative solutions by applying principles from other fields. Her problem-solving speed increased, and she developed a reputation for handling complex technical challenges with ease.

These shifts work because they align with how your brain naturally learns and adapts. They create an environment where neuroplasticity can flourish, leading to enhanced cognitive performance. The key is to approach them not as temporary tactics but as fundamental changes in how you engage your mind each day.

Remember, mental sharpness isn't about being naturally gifted, it's about consistently training your brain in the right ways. These five shifts provide a framework for that training, helping you build a stronger, more agile mind day by day.

Why high achievers think differently—and how you can too

High achievers don't just work differently, they think differently. Their mental patterns and cognitive habits set them apart long before their achievements do. Through decades of cognitive research and real-world observation, we've learned that successful individuals share distinct thinking patterns that drive their performance.

Let's start with pattern recognition. High achievers process information differently by looking for connections where others see chaos. Imagine Samantha, a first-generation entrepreneur who launched a small catering business with big dreams. While others fixated on one-off events, Samantha listened closely to her clients and uncovered a hidden demand for specialized dietary menus. Seeing what others missed, she turned this insight into her advantage, evolving her modest operation into the region's top choice for medical facility catering. Through her vision and intuition, Samantha transformed her business from a local service into a trusted leader meeting a critical need.

The second key difference is their approach to problems. While most people see obstacles as roadblocks, high achievers view them as data points. They break down complex challenges into smaller, manageable components. This systematic thinking allows them to tackle problems that paralyze others.

Consider David, a software engineer confronted with an overwhelming project deadline that would have rattled even the most seasoned professionals. Instead of succumbing to the pressure, he elegantly divided the work into three thoughtful categories: essential features that had to be completed, desirable additions that could enhance the experience, and improvements to be explored in the future. This strategic clarity allowed him to deliver the critical components on time while laying a well-defined foundation for continued growth and refinement.

High achievers also demonstrate superior cognitive flexibility. They readily abandon strategies that don't work, even if they've invested significant time in them. This ability to pivot without emotional attachment to past approaches keeps them adaptable and forward moving.

Isabella embodies this trait in her consulting practice. When traditional in-person workshops became impossible during the corona-virus crisis, she didn't waste time dwelling on the setback. Instead, she quickly pivoted to virtual formats, experimenting with various platforms and techniques until she discovered a model that proved even more effective than her original approach.

Another crucial difference is their relationship with uncertainty. While most people seek certainty before acting, high achievers embrace ambiguity as a source of opportunity. They make decisions with incomplete information, understanding that waiting for perfect clarity often means missing opportunities.

They also practice intentional learning—actively seeking out knowledge gaps rather than avoiding them. When faced with a challenge, they ask themselves: "What do I need to learn to solve this?" rather than "Why can't I solve this?"

But here's the crucial point: these thinking patterns aren't innate talents. They're learned habits that anyone can develop through consistent practice. Here's how you can begin:

- Start breaking down complex problems into smaller components before attempting solutions.
- Practice identifying patterns in everyday situations, from market trends to customer behavior.
- Challenge your assumptions regularly by asking "What if the opposite were true?".
- Embrace uncertainty by taking small, calculated risks with incomplete information.
- Develop a learning mindset by dedicating time each week to explore unfamiliar topics.

The transformation begins with awareness. Pay attention to your current thinking patterns. When facing challenges, notice your instinctive mental responses. Are you seeking immediate solutions or taking time to understand underlying patterns? Are you avoiding uncertainty or viewing it as an opportunity?

Thomas, a mid-level manager transformed his department's performance by adopting these thinking patterns. He started by mapping out recurring problems, looking for connections others had missed. When he noticed that Monday morning meetings were consistently unproductive, he didn't just change the meeting time—he analyzed the pattern and discovered that lack of preparation was the real issue. By implementing a simple pre-meeting review process, he turned these sessions into his team's most valuable collaboration time.

The gap between average and exceptional performance often comes down to these thinking patterns. By consciously adopting and practicing these cognitive habits, you can begin to process information, solve problems, and navigate challenges like high achievers do. The key is consistency—small, daily adjustments in how you think will compound over time, leading to significantly different outcomes.

Your brain is remarkably adaptable. Every time you practice these thinking patterns, you strengthen neural pathways that make this type of thinking more natural and automatic. Start small but start today. Choose one aspect of high achiever thinking and apply it to a current challenge. Notice the difference in how you approach the problem and, more importantly, in the solutions you generate.

Key takeaway: The brain is plastic; the more you train it, the stronger it gets.

Your brain is not fixed—it's constantly changing, rewiring, and strengthening based on how you use it. This remarkable ability, known as neuroplasticity, means your cognitive capabilities aren't set at birth or limited by age. Instead, your brain physically adapts to meet the demands you place on it.

Imagine your brain as a vast network of paths through a forest. Each time you think, learn, or practice a skill, you're walking down one of these paths. The more you travel on a particular route, the clearer and wider that path becomes. Unused paths gradually fade, while frequently used ones develop into superhighways of neural connections.

This isn't just theory—it's a biological fact. When you consistently engage in challenging mental activities, your brain responds by creating new neural connections and strengthening existing ones. Brain imaging studies have shown that taxi drivers in London develop larger hippocampi—the brain region responsible for spatial memory—after years of navigating the city's complex street layout.

Musicians who practice regularly show enhanced development in areas related to motor control and audio processing.

Picture Michael, a software developer who decided to learn Japanese at 40. In the beginning, the unfamiliar characters and sounds felt daunting and almost impossible to grasp. But with just 20 minutes of dedicated practice each morning, his brain slowly began to adapt. After six months, what once seemed like an indecipherable code started to feel familiar and even intuitive. His mind had truly rewired itself to embrace a completely new language.

The key to leveraging neuroplasticity lies in consistent, focused practice. Short, regular training sessions prove more effective than sporadic intense efforts. This explains why spending 30 minutes daily on a challenging mental task yields better results than a single six-hour cramming session.

Your brain also responds to variety. Learning different but related skills creates stronger neural networks than repeatedly practicing the same task. A musician who studies multiple instruments develops more robust musical processing abilities than one who focuses solely on a single instrument.

But here's what many people miss: mental training isn't just about adding new skills, it's about challenging your existing patterns. When you push beyond your comfort zone, tackle unfamiliar problems, or question your assumptions, you're creating new neural pathways that make your brain more adaptable.

Consider Elena, an accountant who felt trapped in rigid, analytical thinking. To shake things up, she signed up for improv comedy classes — an experience that demanded quick thinking and creativity. At first, she felt completely out of her depth. But as she stuck with it, she noticed a shift: her creativity blossomed, and her problem-solving skills at work improved dramatically. By challenging her brain in an entirely new way, she expanded her cognitive flexibility and unlocked unexpected potential.

The implications are clear: your brain's capacity for growth isn't limited by age or natural ability, it's limited by how you train it. Every time you learn something new, solve a complex problem, or push beyond your mental comfort zone, you're building a stronger, more adaptable brain.

This understanding transforms how you should approach personal and professional development. Instead of viewing your capabilities as fixed, recognize that every challenge is an opportunity to strengthen your brain. The more you train it, the stronger it gets—not just in specific skills, but in its overall ability to learn, adapt, and solve problems.

Start treating your brain like the adaptable organ it is. Challenge it regularly. Feed it variety. Push its boundaries. The changes won't be immediate, but they will be real and lasting. Because when it comes to your brain, consistent training doesn't just build skills, it physically reshapes the very organ responsible for your thinking, learning, and growth. The Mental Agility Framework isn't just another set of tips and tricks—it's a fundamental shift in how we approach thinking and decision-making. As we've seen through real examples like Borders' downfall and the rise of adaptable businesses, the quality of our thinking determines the quality of our outcomes.

The five core thinking habits we explored—from embracing productive discomfort to developing cognitive flexibility—are grounded in both cognitive science and practical application. These aren't theoretical concepts, but battle-tested strategies used by those who consistently stay ahead of change.

Consider how differently Borders' story might have ended had its leaders understood and applied these principles. Instead of dismissing e-commerce as a threat, they could have recognized patterns early, challenged their assumptions about consumer behavior, and adapted their business model before it was too late.

The five core thinking habits extend far beyond business strategy. Whether you're navigating career transitions, solving complex problems, or making high-stakes decisions, the Mental Agility Framework provides a practical system for clearer, faster, and more effective thinking.

High achievers think differently not because of innate talent, but because they've developed specific cognitive habits. They break complex problems into manageable components, recognize patterns where others see chaos, and maintain flexibility in their thinking even when faced with uncertainty.

Most importantly, you now understand that these capabilities aren't fixed, they're trainable. Your brain's plasticity means that every time you apply these thinking habits, you're strengthening neural pathways that make this type of thinking more natural and automatic.

CHAPTER 6

THINKING IN THE AI AGE: WHAT MACHINES CAN'T REPLACE

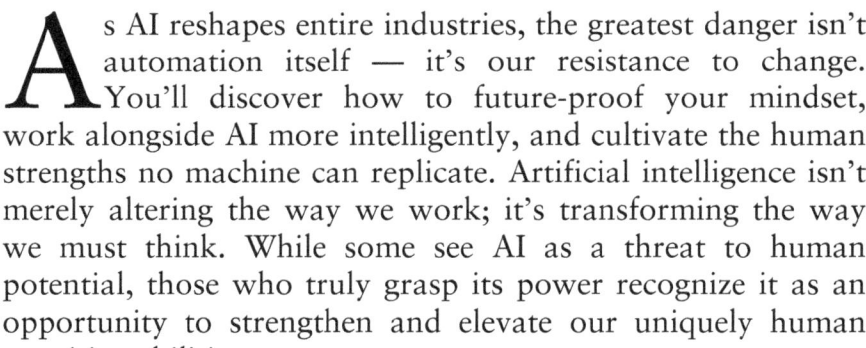

As AI reshapes entire industries, the greatest danger isn't automation itself — it's our resistance to change. You'll discover how to future-proof your mindset, work alongside AI more intelligently, and cultivate the human strengths no machine can replicate. Artificial intelligence isn't merely altering the way we work; it's transforming the way we must think. While some see AI as a threat to human potential, those who truly grasp its power recognize it as an opportunity to strengthen and elevate our uniquely human cognitive abilities.

Imagine the profound shift happening in workplaces across the globe. Just as computers didn't eliminate jobs but transformed them, AI is creating new opportunities for those who learn to leverage it effectively. The key lies not in competing with AI's computational power, but in cultivating the cognitive abilities that machines cannot replicate such as creative problem-solving, emotional intelligence, and adaptive thinking.

For ten years, Lisa was a customer service representative at a large company. She knew the products inside and out, could handle the toughest customers, and took pride in her work.

Then, one day, her manager announced that the company was rolling out AI chatbots to handle most inquiries. The bots were faster, never got tired, and could assist multiple customers at once. Lisa felt panic, what if she was no longer needed? Some of her coworkers ignored the change, hoping it would fail. But Lisa did something different, she learned how to work with AI instead of against it. She started training the chatbot, improving its responses, and using AI to speed up her own work. When layoffs came, the employees who resisted AI were let go, while Lisa was promoted to manage AI-assisted customer experience. She didn't just survive the change—she thrived because of it. Her story is a reminder that AI won't replace people, but it will replace people who refuse to adapt.

This transformation mirrors a broader truth about success in the AI age: it's not about competing with machines—it's about complementing them. The most successful professionals aren't those who try to outperform AI at its strengths, but those who develop mental agility to work alongside it, leveraging its capabilities while honing their distinctly human advantages.

We'll explore the cognitive skills that AI can't replicate — and why developing these abilities is vital for long-term success. You'll uncover practical strategies to enhance your creative thinking, strengthen your emotional intelligence, and build adaptive problem-solving skills that will remain essential no matter how technology evolves.

The goal isn't to resist AI or fear its advancement, it's to understand how to think better in a world where artificial intelligence is becoming increasingly prevalent.

AI is changing the game, but human thinking still matters

While artificial intelligence excels at processing vast amounts of data and identifying patterns, human cognition remains uniquely powerful in ways that machines cannot replicate. Our ability to draw novel connections, understand context, and apply emotional intelligence gives us distinct advantages that complement rather than compete with AI.

Consider how a chess grandmaster approaches the game differently from a chess computer. While AI can calculate millions of possible moves per second, human players rely on intuition, pattern recognition, and strategic thinking that have been developed through years of experience. This combination of analytical and intuitive thinking allows humans to make creative moves that sometimes surprise even the most sophisticated chess engines.

The key to thriving in an AI-driven world lies in developing cognitive abilities that machines don't possess. These include:

- Contextual Understanding: Grasping nuance and meaning beyond literal interpretation.
- Creative Problem-Solving: Generating novel solutions to unprecedented challenges.
- Emotional Intelligence: Reading social cues and navigating complex human relationships.
- Strategic Thinking: Making decisions based on incomplete information and changing circumstances.

Harper, a radiologist who initially feared that AI might render her profession obsolete, chose not to resist the technology but to embrace it and learn to work alongside it. While AI enabled her to screen images more quickly and detect subtle abnormalities, Harper's medical expertise, her skill in communicating with patients, and her ability to consider the unique context of each case became even more essential. She could explain complex diagnoses with compassion, integrate patients' medical histories and lifestyle factors into treatment plans, and make nuanced decisions that AI couldn't handle on its own.

This partnership between human intelligence and artificial intelligence represents the future of cognitive work. AI handles repetitive tasks and data processing, freeing humans to focus on higher-order thinking, creativity, and complex decision-making. The most successful professionals will be those who understand how to leverage both.

The human brain's plasticity—its ability to adapt, learn, and form new neural connections—gives us an advantage that current AI systems lack. While machines are programmed with fixed algorithms, we can continuously evolve our thinking patterns, develop new skills, and adapt to changing circumstances.

Developing these uniquely human cognitive abilities requires deliberate practice. Just as athletes train their bodies, we must train our minds to think more deeply, creatively, and adaptively. This means challenging ourselves with complex problems, seeking out diverse perspectives, and regularly pushing beyond our cognitive comfort zones.

The future belongs to those who understand how to think alongside AI. By focusing on developing our distinctly human cognitive advantages, creativity, emotional intelligence, and adaptive thinking, we ensure our relevance in an increasingly automated world. The goal isn't to compete with machines at their strengths, but to cultivate the mental capabilities that make us uniquely human.

The 3 cognitive skills AI can't replicate—and how to master them

While artificial intelligence continues to advance at a remarkable pace, three fundamental cognitive abilities remain uniquely human: adaptive creativity, contextual decision-making, and empathetic reasoning. These skills form the core of human intelligence that machines, despite their computational power, cannot truly replicate.

Adrian, a product designer who initially feared that AI might render his role obsolete, soon realized that design software could now generate hundreds of variations in seconds and image-generation tools could create visuals from simple text prompts. However, he discovered that his actual value didn't lie in the mechanical aspects of "design" but in his ability to understand the deeper human elements of his work.

The first irreplaceable skill is adaptive creativity, the ability to generate novel solutions by connecting seemingly unrelated concepts and experiences. Unlike AI, which can only combine existing patterns in its training data, humans can make intuitive leaps based on diverse life experiences, emotions, and abstract thinking. Adrian used this ability to design products that addressed unspoken human needs, something no AI could identify through data alone.

You can develop adaptive creativity through:
- Exposing yourself to diverse experiences and fields of knowledge.
- Practicing connecting disparate ideas in unexpected ways.
- Challenging assumptions about conventional solutions.
- Embracing constraints as catalysts for innovation.

The second cognitive skill machines can't match is contextual decision-making—understanding the nuanced implications of choices within complex social and emotional frameworks. While AI excels at analyzing data points, it cannot grasp the subtle cultural, emotional, and interpersonal dynamics that influence human decisions.

Claire, a negotiation specialist who works with both AI analysis tools and human clients, relies on technology to process contract terms and suggest optimal deals based on historical data. However, her true strength lies in reading body language, uncovering hidden motivations, and navigating cultural nuances — abilities that demand deep human intuition and insight.

To strengthen contextual decision-making:

- Practice considering multiple perspectives in every situation.
- Study the broader implications of decisions beyond immediate outcomes.
- Develop awareness of cultural and emotional factors.
- Learn from direct human interaction and observation.

The third uniquely human capability is empathetic reasoning—the ability to truly understand and respond to others' emotional states, needs, and motivations. This goes beyond simple pattern recognition of facial expressions or voice tones that AI can perform. It involves understanding the complex web of human experiences, emotions, and relationships that shape behavior.

Max, a teacher who uses AI to help grade assignments and create lesson plans, found that his most important skill was building emotional connections with students. While AI could identify learning patterns and suggest interventions, only Max could notice a student's subtle change in confidence, understand family dynamics affecting performance, or provide the kind of encouragement that resonates on a personal level.

To enhance empathetic reasoning:

- Actively practice perspective-taking in daily interactions.
- Develop deep listening skills beyond just hearing words.
- Study human psychology and emotional intelligence.
- Engage in activities that require understanding others' experiences.

These three cognitive skills—adaptive creativity, contextual decision-making, and empathetic reasoning—form the foundation of human intelligence that AI cannot replicate. They represent our unique ability to understand context, create novel connections, and deeply comprehend human experience.

The key to mastering these skills is not in competing with AI, but in developing abilities that complement it. By focusing on these distinctly human capabilities, we can create value that machines cannot replicate, ensuring our relevance in an increasingly automated world.

Remember, the goal isn't to resist technological advancement but to cultivate the cognitive abilities that make us uniquely human. As AI continues to evolve, these skills will become even more valuable, creating opportunities for those who develop them effectively.

Real-world example: Why Steve Jobs, Jeff Bezos, and top innovators focus on agile thinking.

When Steve Jobs returned to Apple in 1997, he found a company drowning in complexity—dozens of computer models, confusing product lines, and scattered focus. Instead of following conventional business wisdom to diversify, Jobs did something radical: he eliminated 70% of Apple's products. This wasn't just about streamlining—it demonstrated the power of mental agility in leadership.

Jobs understood that success in technology wasn't about having the most products or following industry trends; it was about creating innovative solutions. It required the ability to anticipate change, challenge assumptions, and make bold decisions quickly. He reduced Apple's product line to just four computers, focusing the company's resources and creativity on making them exceptional. This decision, while controversial at the time, laid the foundation for Apple's transformation from a struggling computer maker into one of the world's most valuable companies.

This pattern of mental agility driving innovation repeats across the tech industry. Jeff Bezos built Amazon's culture around what he calls "Day 1 thinking," approaching each day with the adaptability and urgency of a startup, regardless of the company's size. This mindset helped Amazon evolve from an online bookstore into a global technology leader, pioneering innovations in cloud computing, voice-controlled AI, and more.

These leaders share a common trait: they don't just react to change—they anticipate and shape it. They maintain what psychologists call cognitive flexibility—the ability to switch between different modes of thinking and adapt strategies based on new information. This isn't just about being smart; it's about being mentally agile.

Consider how this plays out in practice. When Apple developed the iPhone, Jobs didn't just create a better phone, he reimagined what a phone could be. This required breaking free from established thinking about mobile devices and envisioning an entirely new category of products. Similarly, when Bezos launched Amazon Web Services, he had to think beyond Amazon's identity as a retailer to see the future of cloud computing.

But mental agility isn't just for tech innovators. It's becoming essential across all industries as technology and market conditions evolve at an accelerating pace. Leaders who maintain fixed mindsets or rely on outdated strategies increasingly find themselves falling behind, while those who cultivate thinking agility can spot opportunities others miss.

The key components of thinking agility that these innovators practice include:

- Questioning fundamental assumptions about their industry.
- Remaining open to contradictory evidence.
- Making decisive moves based on emerging patterns.
- Adapting strategies quickly when conditions change.
- Maintaining focus while staying open to new possibilities.

This thinking approach has become even more crucial in today's rapidly changing business environment. The ability to process new information quickly, challenge existing assumptions, and adapt strategies in real-time often matters more than traditional business metrics.

The lesson from these innovators is clear: mental agility isn't just a valuable skill—it's a fundamental requirement for success in a world of constant change. They show that the most valuable asset in business isn't knowledge or resources, but the ability to think flexibly and adapt quickly when circumstances demand it.

This focus on thinking agility has practical implications for anyone looking to succeed in today's environment. It suggests that we should spend less time trying to predict the future and more time developing mental flexibility to adapt to whatever comes. The goal isn't to know everything but to maintain the cognitive agility to learn and adapt as needed.

The examples of Jobs, Bezos, and other innovators show that mental agility isn't just about being intelligent or knowledgeable; it's about maintaining the flexibility to see things differently when circumstances change. This capacity for adaptive thinking, more than any specific skill or knowledge, defines success in an era of rapid change.

Lisa's story of transforming her customer service role illustrates a fundamental truth: success in an AI-driven world stems from developing cognitive abilities that machines cannot replicate. As artificial intelligence handles increasingly complex computational tasks, our value lies in adaptive creativity, contextual decision-making, and empathetic reasoning—skills that remain uniquely human.

The evidence is compelling. While AI can process vast amounts of data and identify patterns, it cannot match our ability to draw novel connections, understand nuanced context, or navigate the complex landscape of human emotions. The radiologist who learns to work alongside AI, enhancing rather than resisting its capabilities, shows us a model for the future—one where human intelligence and artificial intelligence complement each other.

Let's be clear: AI isn't eliminating the need for human thinking—it's elevating its importance. As routine tasks become automated, our capacity for creative problem-solving, emotional intelligence, and adaptive thinking becomes more crucial. The most successful individuals and organizations will be those who understand this shift and invest in developing these distinctly human cognitive abilities.

We've explored how leaders across industries are already demonstrating this principle. From product designers who combine AI's computational power with human creativity to negotiation specialists who blend data analysis with emotional intelligence, the pattern is clear: mental agility in the AI age means knowing when to leverage technology and when to rely on uniquely human capabilities.

The key isn't to fear AI or compete with it, but to understand how it can enhance our thinking while we focus on strengthening the cognitive abilities that machines cannot replicate. This is the path to remaining relevant and valuable in an increasingly automated world.

The future doesn't belong to the machines. It belongs to those who understand how to think alongside them.

CHAPTER 7

HOW TO STAY AHEAD WHEN THE RULES KEEP CHANGING

The world is changing faster than ever, and those who cling to old ways of thinking will be left behind, just as businesses that failed to anticipate the rise of the internet were. Learn to anticipate change, adapt before you're forced to, and cultivate a mindset that keeps you ahead of the curve—just like Jeff Bezos did when he built Amazon long before the world even realized it needed it. This reality becomes even clearer when we look at how quickly entire industries can transform. The companies that dominate today's markets aren't necessarily the ones with the most resources or the longest history, they're the ones that spotted shifts early and adapted fastest. While others wait for change to force their hand, successful organizations and individuals actively scan the horizon, identifying emerging trends and preparing for multiple scenarios.

In the early 1990s, Jeff Bezos demonstrated this principle perfectly. Working on Wall Street, he noticed staggering statistics: the internet was growing at a rate of 2,300% per year. Most people dismissed this as a temporary trend, but Bezos saw more profound implications. He recognized that this exponential growth would fundamentally reshape how people bought and sold goods. Instead of clinging to his secure Wall Street career, he acted decisively, moving to Seattle to start an online bookstore from his garage.

At the time, traditional bookstores dominated the market. Critics scoffed at the idea that people would purchase books without physically holding them first. But Bezos wasn't playing by old rules—he was anticipating new ones. That small online bookstore became Amazon, revolutionizing not just book sales but the entire retail industry.

The lesson here isn't just about spotting opportunities, it's about developing the mental agility to recognize when the rules of the game are changing. In today's rapid-paced world, success depends less on what you know and more on how quickly you can learn, adapt, and implement new strategies. The organizations and individuals who thrive aren't necessarily the strongest or most knowledgeable, they're the ones who stay mentally flexible and adjust course before change becomes unavoidable.

When patterns shift, many people's first instinct is to defend established practices or ignore warning signs. This resistance to change, while natural, can be fatal in both business and personal growth. The key is developing a mindset that not only responds to change but also anticipates and welcomes it. This means constantly questioning assumptions, staying curious about emerging trends, and being willing to abandon strategies that no longer serve their purpose.

Consider how streaming transformed entertainment, how smartphones revolutionized communication, or how artificial intelligence is reshaping every industry. These weren't sudden changes—they emerged gradually, with clear signals that most people chose to ignore. The winners in each case weren't those who waited for disruption to become obvious, but those who prepared early and positioned themselves ahead of the curve.

Why success is not about what you know—but how fast you can adapt

In 1995, a young software developer named Larissa Martinez had mastered every programming language available. She worked at a leading tech company, wrote flawless code, and knew the industry inside out. But within five years, half of what she knew became obsolete. New languages emerged, development frameworks evolved, and the way software was built underwent dramatic changes. Her colleagues who clung to their existing knowledge struggled, while Larissa took a different approach—she focused on becoming an expert at learning rather than an expert at knowing.

Instead of resisting new technologies, Larissa developed a system to learn and implement them quickly. When cloud computing emerged, she was among the first to understand its implications. When mobile development took off, she pivoted before her company even had a mobile strategy. Her value wasn't in what she knew—it was in how fast she could adapt to what she didn't know.

This pattern repeats across every industry and profession. The skills that make someone successful today might become irrelevant tomorrow. Traditional education teaches us to accumulate knowledge, but in a rapidly changing world, the ability to unlearn and relearn matters more than the information we currently possess.

Reflect on how work has evolved in recent years. Remote collaboration tools, artificial intelligence, and automation have reshaped entire industries. The professionals who thrive aren't necessarily the most knowledgeable, they're the ones who adapt fastest to new tools, methods, and ways of working.

The key is developing what psychologists call 'learning agility'—the ability to learn, unlearn, and relearn quickly. This means approaching every situation with curiosity rather than certainty. It means questioning assumptions, experimenting with new approaches, and being willing to abandon practices that no longer serve their purpose.

Think of your mind like a computer's operating system. Having a large amount of stored data (knowledge) is useful, but what's more important is having a fast processor that can quickly download, integrate, and apply new information. The most successful people don't just accumulate information—they build mental frameworks that help them process and adapt to new situations rapidly.

This shift from knowledge-based success to adaptation-based success requires a fundamental change in how we approach learning and growth. Instead of asking 'What do I need to know?' start asking 'How quickly can I learn what I need?' Rather than measuring success by what you've mastered, measure it by how effectively you can tackle unfamiliar challenges.

The good news is that adaptability, like any skill, can be developed. It starts with embracing uncertainty as an opportunity rather than a threat. When you encounter new situations, resist the urge to rely solely on past knowledge. Instead, approach them with fresh eyes, ready to learn and adjust your thinking.

Practice makes this easier. Start small—try learning something completely new each month. It could be new technology, a different approach to problem-solving, or an unfamiliar way of working. The goal isn't mastery; it's building the mental muscles that make adaptation easier.

Remember Larissa? Today, she leads innovation at her company, not because she knows everything, but because she's mastered the art of learning anything. Her story reminds us that in a world of constant change, the most valuable skill isn't knowledge, it's the ability to adapt when that knowledge becomes outdated.

This shift in thinking—from valuing what you know to valuing how fast you can adapt—is crucial for long-term success. Those who master this skill don't just survive change; they thrive because of it. They turn disruption into opportunity and uncertainty into advantage.

How to learn, unlearn, and relearn faster than anyone else

In 1956, IBM introduced the first hard disk drive, which was the size of two refrigerators, weighed over a ton, and stored only 5MB of data. Today, we carry a thousand times more storage in our pockets. This transformation didn't occur through gradual improvement—it required a complete rethink of how we store information. The engineers who led these breakthroughs weren't just learning new techniques; they were actively unlearning old assumptions about what was possible.

This principle extends far beyond technology. The most successful professionals today aren't those who accumulate knowledge—they're the ones who can rapidly learn, unlearn outdated information, and relearn new approaches. They understand that expertise isn't just about adding new skills; it's about letting go of obsolete ones.

Meet Lee Chen, a software architect who transformed his approach to learning when he realized traditional methods weren't keeping pace with technology changes. Instead of trying to memorize every new programming language or framework, he developed a three-part system: rapid learning, strategic unlearning, and focused relearning.

For rapid learning, Lee breaks down complex topics into fundamental principles. Rather than memorizing specific solutions, he identifies underlying patterns. This approach helps him grasp new concepts quickly because he's not starting from scratch; instead, he builds on core principles that remain constant.

Strategic unlearning proved more challenging. It required actively identifying and abandoning practices that no longer served their purpose. When cloud computing emerged, Lee had to unlearn deeply ingrained habits about server management and security. This wasn't just about learning new tools—it meant deliberately setting aside knowledge he'd spent years acquiring.

Focused relearning combines the previous steps. Once Lee identifies outdated knowledge and core principles, he can rapidly acquire new skills that align with current needs. This isn't about starting over; it's about building new expertise on a foundation of fundamental understanding.

Here's how you can apply this three-part system:

- Start with fundamentals: Before getting into specific tools or techniques, understand the basic principles behind them. These rarely change and provide a framework for faster learning.
- Question your assumptions: Regularly examine your current practices. Ask yourself: "What if this approach is

no longer the best way? What alternatives might work better?"
- Build learning frameworks: Create systems that help you process new information quickly. This might include mind mapping, teaching others, or practical applications.

The key is maintaining intellectual humility. Recognize that today's expertise might become tomorrow's obstacle. This doesn't mean dismissing experience, it means holding knowledge lightly enough to update it if and when necessary.

Consider how doctors must constantly update their medical knowledge. New research regularly challenges established treatments. The best physicians aren't those who cling to what they learned in medical school, they're the ones who stay current by continuously learning, unlearning outdated practices, and relearning based on new evidence.

This approach requires a fundamental shift in how we view expertise. Instead of seeing it as a destination where we've 'mastered' something, we should view it as a continuous journey of adaptation. The goal isn't to know everything; it's to develop systems that help us learn anything.

Practical steps for faster learning and adaptation:

- Focus on understanding rather than memorization.
- Test new knowledge through immediate application.
- Teach concepts to others to reinforce understanding.
- Regularly review and update existing knowledge.
- Seek feedback and adjust approaches accordingly.

Remember, the goal isn't to become an expert in everything; it's to develop the ability to quickly become competent in what matters most. This requires both the humility to acknowledge when our current knowledge is outdated and the confidence to tackle new challenges.

By mastering the cycle of learning, unlearning, and relearning, you develop a sustainable approach to growth that keeps you ahead of change rather than struggling to catch up. This isn't just about professional success; it's about maintaining relevance and effectiveness in a world where the only certainty is that tomorrow's challenges will be different from today's.

Exercise: The "Mental Reset" Technique for adapting to change instantly

When faced with sudden change, most people freeze. Their minds get stuck processing what they've lost instead of adapting to what's possible. The Mental Reset Technique breaks this pattern by creating an instant shift in perspective and action. This evidence-based approach combines elements of cognitive reframing with rapid implementation strategies.

The technique consists of three simple steps that take less than 60 seconds to execute:

- Acknowledge Reality: Take 10 seconds to state the situation exactly as it is, without emotion or judgment
- Identify Options: Spend 20 seconds listing 2-3 immediate actions you can take
- Choose and Move: Take 30 seconds to select one action and begin implementing it

Let's see this technique in action through the story of Maya, a digital marketing specialist. During a crucial client presentation, her carefully prepared slides crashed. Instead of panicking, she applied the Mental Reset:

10 seconds: 'The presentation software isn't working. This is the current reality.' 20 seconds – Options:

1) Draw key points on the whiteboard,
2) Tell client stories without visuals,
3) Email presentation and walk-through verbally 30 seconds: Chose option two and began sharing case studies conversationally.

The result? Her client appreciated the authentic approach, and she landed the contract. The technique worked because it bypassed the natural tendency to resist change and moved straight to adaptation.

To master the Mental Reset Technique, start by practicing it with small changes. When your regular coffee shop is closed, your usual route to work is blocked, or a meeting gets canceled, use these moments as opportunities to strengthen your ability to adapt. The goal isn't to ignore discomfort but to move through it productively.

Here's a practical exercise to build this skill:

- Set a timer for 60 seconds
- Write down a recent change that disrupted your plans
- Apply the three steps: Acknowledge, Identify, Choose
- Immediately take the action you selected

Do this exercise three times this week with different scenarios. Each time, notice how the speed of your adaptation improves. The power of this technique lies in its simplicity and immediate application. It doesn't require special tools or ideal conditions - just a willingness to act quickly when circumstances change.

Remember, the objective isn't to become immune to the impact of change, but to reduce the gap between disruption and response. Every time you practice the Mental Reset, you're strengthening neural pathways that make adaptation easier. This isn't just about professional situations - the technique works equally well for personal challenges, relationship dynamics, and daily obstacles.

The key is consistency. Make the Mental Reset your default response to unexpected changes, instead of wasting energy resisting what has happened, channel that energy into rapid adaptation. Over time, you'll notice that changes that once derailed you for hours now only impact you for minutes.

Start small but practice regularly. The next time an unexpected change occurs, time yourself applying the technique. Notice how quickly you can move from acknowledgment to action. With practice, this reset becomes almost automatic, giving you a significant advantage in situations where others might still be processing the initial shock of change.

The Mental Reset Technique transforms change from a source of stress into a trigger for focused action. It's not about pretending disruption doesn't affect you - it's about developing the mental agility to adapt and move forward regardless of circumstances. This skill, once mastered, becomes invaluable in both professional and personal contexts, allowing you to maintain momentum even when faced with unexpected obstacles. The future won't wait for those who hesitate. In today's rapidly evolving landscape, mental agility isn't just an advantage; it's essential for survival.

We've examined the critical components of adaptability through real-world examples and practical frameworks. From Jeff Bezos's early recognition of the internet's transformative power to Sarah Martinez's systematic approach to continuous learning, we've seen how mental flexibility translates into tangible success. These stories illustrate a fundamental truth: success isn't determined by what you know, but by how quickly you can adapt when that knowledge becomes obsolete.

The Mental Reset Technique provides a practical tool for instant adaptation, while the three-part system of learning, unlearning, and relearning offers a structured approach to continuous growth. These aren't theoretical concepts—they're battle-tested strategies used by professionals across industries to navigate uncertainty and seize opportunities others miss.

But perhaps the most important lesson is this: adaptability isn't a trait you're born with—it's a skill you can develop. Through consistent practice and the right mental frameworks, anyone can enhance their ability to think flexibly, adapt quickly, and make more informed decisions under pressure.

As you move forward, remember that staying ahead isn't about predicting the future perfectly—it's about developing mental agility to respond effectively when circumstances change. Your success tomorrow depends on the mental habits you build today.

The world won't slow down, but with the right mindset and tools, you can develop the mental agility to thrive in its constant evolution. The question isn't whether change will come—it's whether you'll be prepared when it does.

CHAPTER 8

DECISION MAKING UNDER PRESSURE

Navy SEALs who succeed don't just rely on physical strength; they employ mental strategies like setting micro-goals, practicing controlled breathing, and maintaining relentless focus to push beyond their limits. We'll review and learn how to apply these same techniques to develop unshakable resilience, discipline, and mental agility, preparing you to handle any challenge life throws your way. These techniques aren't just abstract concepts, they're battle-tested strategies that work under the most extreme conditions imaginable. When lives hang in the balance, when split-second decisions determine success or failure, having a trained mind is a prized asset.

But decision-making under pressure isn't just for military operators. Every day, business leaders face market shifts that demand immediate action. Healthcare professionals make life-altering choices in emergency rooms. And regular people navigate critical moments that shape their futures, from career moves to relationship challenges.

Like the elite operators who face life-or-death situations, we can train our minds to function optimally when stakes are high, and time is short. The key lies in understanding how pressure affects our thinking and developing specific mental tools to maintain clarity when others lose focus.

Becoming a U.S. Navy SEAL isn't just about physical endurance—it's about mental toughness, adaptability, and the ability to stay focused under extreme pressure. Every SEAL candidate must survive Hell Week, a grueling five-day test where they endure continuous physical training on less than four hours of sleep, freezing ocean swims, and relentless obstacle courses designed to push them to their absolute limit. Many are strong, but most fail—not because their bodies give out, but because their minds break first.

The ones who succeed are those who train their thinking, mastering emotional control, resilience, and the ability to embrace discomfort. They use micro-goals to stay focused, breaking the pain down into manageable minutes instead of days, and reframe suffering as a challenge rather than a threat. This relentless mental training transforms them into warriors who can operate in chaos, overcome impossible odds, and keep moving forward no matter how difficult the mission.

Their training proves that mental strength isn't innate—it's cultivated through specific practices and principles. In this chapter, we'll break down these techniques and show you how to apply them to your challenges. You'll learn practical strategies for maintaining mental clarity under pressure, making confident decisions when stakes are high, and developing the kind of resilience that turns obstacles into opportunities.

Whether you're leading a team through a crisis, making career-defining choices, or facing personal challenges, these tools will help you think clearly when pressure mounts. Because in our rapidly changing world, the ability to make wise decisions under stress isn't just helpful—it's essential for survival and success.

The 3-step formula for handling high-pressure decisions.

When pressure mounts and decisions loom, our brains often default to fight-or-flight mode, clouding judgment and leading to choices we later regret. By studying how experienced decision-makers maintain clarity under extreme conditions, we can identify a reliable three-step approach that cuts through the chaos and leads to better outcomes.

Step 1: Pause and OrientThe first crucial step is creating mental space between the trigger and your response. Take three deep breaths while asking yourself: "What's happening right now?" This brief pause interrupts the automatic stress response and activates your prefrontal cortex—the brain's command center for rational thinking.

This isn't about lengthy meditation or extensive analysis. It's a tactical pause, like a pilot scanning their instruments before making a critical maneuver. During these few seconds, you're not trying to solve the problem, you're simply gathering your bearings and preventing emotion from hijacking your decision-making process.

Step 2: Frame the Core DecisionAfter the pause, strip away all the noise and identify the essential choice at hand. Ask: "What's the one decision that matters most right now?" Often, what feels like a complex problem can be reduced to a single critical choice.

For example, Mona, a startup founder, faced a crisis when her main competitor suddenly slashed prices by 50%. Her team bombarded her with various concerns and suggested responses. But she used this step to frame the core decision:

"Do we match their pricing or maintain our premium positioning?" This clarity helped her focus on what truly mattered, rather than getting lost in reactive planning.

Step 3: Run the Fast-Forward Test Once you've identified the core decision, project yourself into the future and ask: "Which choice will I be proud of one year from now?" This future-focused perspective helps bypass temporary emotions and align decisions with long-term values.

This isn't about predicting outcomes, it's about ensuring your choice reflects your principles rather than just immediate pressures. The fast-forward test often reveals that what feels urgent in the moment may not align with what's truly important.

This three-step model is simple and effective. Under pressure, complex frameworks fall apart. You need something you can easily recall and instantly apply. Each step serves a specific purpose: the pause prevents reactive decisions, the framing creates clarity, and the fast-forward test ensures alignment with your values.

Consider Alexander, an emergency room physician who regularly faces life-or-death decisions. When a critical patient arrives with unusual symptoms, he uses this exact formula. He takes a quick pause to orient himself, frames the core decision about immediate treatment priorities, and considers which choice he could confidently defend during case review. This systematic approach helps him maintain clarity even in chaotic situations.

The key is to practice this formula in lower-stakes situations so that it becomes an automatic response. Start with daily decisions, like responding to challenging emails or handling unexpected work conflicts. With practice, this three-step approach becomes a mental reflex, ready to deploy when you need it most.

Remember, the point isn't to get rid of pressure; it's to maintain clear thinking no matter how intense it gets.

This formula provides a reliable framework for making informed decisions when stakes are high and time is limited. By following these steps, you transform pressure from a source of stress into a catalyst for better decision-making.

How to train your brain for clarity under stress

Training your brain to maintain clarity under stress isn't about eliminating pressure, it's about building mental systems that function effectively despite it. Like a pilot practicing emergency procedures in a flight simulator, you can develop specific mental routines that kick in automatically when pressure mounts.

The foundation of mental clarity under stress lies in understanding how your brain processes pressure. When faced with stress, your amygdala—the brain's threat detection center—can override your prefrontal cortex, the region responsible for logical thinking. This 'amygdala hijack' evolved to help our ancestors survive immediate physical threats, but it can impair decision-making in modern high-pressure situations.

To counter this natural response, start with controlled breathing exercises. The technique used by combat operators is called box breathing: inhale for four counts, hold for four, exhale for four counts, and hold for four. This pattern activates your parasympathetic nervous system, reducing stress hormones and allowing for clearer thinking.

Mark, a trauma surgeon, uses this technique before every complex procedure. "Between seeing the patient and making the first incision, I take 30 seconds for box breathing. It's not meditation, it's mental preparation. Those breaths clear the static and sharpen my focus."

Beyond breathing, build stress inoculation through progressive exposure. Start with small challenges and gradually increase intensity. For instance, practice making decisions with artificial time constraints. Set a timer for two minutes to solve a work problem. Then reduce it to one minute. Eventually, 30 seconds. This isn't about rushing, it's about maintaining mental clarity under increasing pressure.

Another powerful technique is scenario planning. Before important events, visualize three possible outcomes: best case, worst case, and most likely case. This mental rehearsal reduces uncertainty and builds confidence in your ability to handle various situations. Elite performers use this method to prepare for high-stakes moments, ensuring their thinking remains clear when pressure peaks.

Develop a personal stress protocol—a series of actions you take when pressure intensifies. Kasimira, a corporate negotiator, employs what she calls the '3R Method': Reset (perform two box breaths), Review (state the core issue aloud), and Respond (take one decisive action). Having this protocol prevents mental paralysis during crucial moments.

Regular practice in lower-stakes situations builds neural pathways that activate automatically under pressure. It's like building muscle memory for your mind. The key is consistency—train these techniques daily, not just during crises.

Remember, stress isn't your enemy. The right amount of pressure can enhance performance by increasing focus and motivation. The goal is to harness stress while maintaining mental clarity. This balance comes from understanding your optimal pressure point, the level of stress that energizes rather than overwhelms.

Incorporate physical movement into your stress response. Simple actions like standing up straight, rolling your shoulders back, or taking a few steps can break the cycle of mental tension and restore clear thinking. These movements signal to your brain that you're taking control rather than freezing under pressure.

Lastly, maintain perspective through micro-goals. When stress mounts, break challenges into smaller, manageable pieces. Instead of obsessing on the entire problem, focus on the next immediate step. This approach prevents mental overwhelm and keeps your thinking sharp when the stakes are high.

Real-world example: What Navy SEALs and top CEOs do when faced with split-second choices

When lives hang in the balance, both Navy SEALs and top executives rely on similar mental frameworks to make split-second decisions. While their contexts differ dramatically, their core decision-making processes share remarkable similarities.

In combat situations, Navy SEALs employ a technique known as "mental rehearsal" to prepare for critical moments. Before missions, they visualize various scenarios and pre-plan their responses. This mental preparation allows them to act decisively when split seconds matter. They focus on identifying the critical factors that determine success or failure, eliminating unnecessary variables that could cloud judgment.

The same principle applies in corporate leadership. Jamie Yang, the CEO of a major tech company, faced a server crash that threatened to disrupt service for millions of users. Instead of getting caught in the panic, she applied a decision-making framework similar to that of military operators: assess the situation quickly, identify the critical path, and take decisive action. Within minutes, she had authorized an emergency protocol that saved the company millions in potential losses.

Both SEALs and executives understand that hesitation often poses a greater risk than imperfect action. They rely on what psychologists call "recognition-primed decision making" - a pattern recognition based on experience that allows for rapid and effective choices under pressure.

Consider the story of Jordan, a former SEAL who transitioned into business consulting. When one of his clients faced a hostile takeover, he recognized familiar patterns. "Whether in combat or the boardroom, success depends on staying clear-headed when everyone else is losing their nerve," he explains. "You need frameworks that activate instinctively when the pressure is highest."

These frameworks typically include three elements: rapid situation assessment, immediate action planning, and continuous adaptation. SEALs refer to this as the "OODA loop" - Observe, Orient, Decide, Act. Successful executives often employ similar cycles, although they may use different terminology.

The key difference lies not in the framework but in the stakes. While SEALs deal with life-and-death situations, executives face financial and organizational consequences. Yet both groups succeed by training their minds to process information quickly and act decisively when others might freeze.

Jessica Torres, a crisis management expert, implemented these military-inspired decision-making techniques at her consulting firm. During a major product recall, her team used rapid assessment protocols similar to those used by special forces. They broke down complex situations into essential elements, made quick decisions based on available information, and adjusted their course as new data emerged.

This approach differs markedly from traditional business decision-making, which often emphasizes extensive analysis and consensus-building. In high-pressure situations, both SEALs and successful executives understand that perfect information is impossible. They focus instead on making the best decision possible with available data, then adapting as circumstances change.

The lesson isn't about rushing decisions but about developing the mental clarity to act decisively under pressure. Through consistent training and practical frameworks, anyone can develop this capability. It starts with understanding that clear thinking under pressure isn't an innate talent—it's a skill developed through deliberate practice and proper mental preparation. As we've seen, decision-making under pressure isn't just about quick reactions, it's about developing systems that allow your mind to operate effectively when the stakes are highest. From the Navy SEALs' rigorous mental conditioning to the practical frameworks used by leaders in crisis, we've seen how clarity under pressure comes from preparation, practice, and proven methods.

The three-step formula for handling high-pressure decisions provides a reliable structure that cuts through chaos. By learning to pause and orient, frame core decisions, and use the fast-forward test, you build a mental toolkit that serves you in any high-stakes situation. Combined with stress management techniques like box breathing and scenario planning, these tools transform pressure from a source of mental paralysis into a catalyst for decisive action.

But perhaps the most important lesson is that mental clarity under stress isn't a natural talent, it's a trainable skill. Through consistent practice of the techniques we've covered, from controlled breathing to progressive exposure training, anyone can develop the ability to think clearly when pressure mounts. The key is to start small, build gradually, and create mental routines that become automatic when challenges arise.

Remember Alexander, the physician who applied these principles in the emergency room? His story illustrates how systematic approaches to decision-making can be effective in real-world situations where lives are at stake. By breaking down complex choices into manageable steps and maintaining mental clarity through practiced routines, he transformed high-pressure moments from sources of stress into opportunities for effective action.

As you move forward, focus on implementing these tools in your daily life. Start with small decisions, practice the techniques regularly, and gradually increase the stakes as your mental resilience grows. Whether you're leading a team through a crisis, making career-defining choices, or navigating personal challenges, the principles you've learned provide a foundation for clear thinking under pressure.

CHAPTER 9

THE 30-DAY MENTAL UPGRADE PLAN

Great leaders don't bend to fear or allow uncertainty to paralyze them. We'll learn how Jeff Bezos made one of Amazon's most significant decisions under pressure and how you can apply the same mental strategies to think and act decisively and stay ahead in high-stakes situations. This mindset is what separates visionary leaders from those who merely manage. It's about developing the mental clarity to see beyond immediate risks and focus on transformative opportunities, even when the stakes are highest.

Bezos exemplified this through one of Amazon's most pivotal decisions—the launch of Amazon Web Services (AWS). In the early 2000s, while Amazon was flourishing as an online retailer, Bezos recognized a hidden opportunity in cloud computing. The company had built sophisticated internal systems for managing its vast digital infrastructure, and Bezos saw the potential to transform this internal tool into a revolutionary service.

At the time, this decision was subject to intense scrutiny. Amazon was primarily known for selling books and consumer goods, not providing technology infrastructure. The move would require billions in investment, with no guarantee of success. Even Amazon's executives questioned whether businesses would trust a retailer to provide critical tech services over established giants like IBM and Microsoft.

But instead of getting paralyzed by analysis or succumbing to doubt, Bezos applied a straightforward decision-making framework: "If I fast-forward 10 years, will I regret NOT doing this?" This mental model cut through the complexity and fear, providing a crystal-clear focus for the decision.

The result? AWS became not just successful but transformative, both for Amazon and the entire technology landscape. Today, it powers everything from Netflix to NASA, generating more profit than Amazon's retail operations. What seemed like a risky deviation from Amazon's core business became the foundation of its future.

Here, we'll break down the mental frameworks that enable clear thinking under pressure. You'll learn practical techniques for cutting through fear and uncertainty, methods for evaluating high-stakes decisions, and strategies for maintaining mental clarity when others become clouded by emotion or hesitation.

Authentic leadership isn't about avoiding pressure—it's about developing the mental tools to think clearly and act decisively when pressure is highest. Whether you're making business decisions, personal choices, or navigating life's challenges, these frameworks will give you the mental clarity to act with confidence and purpose.

We'll explore specific techniques for developing this clarity, from the 3-Second Rule for quick decisions to advanced frameworks for complex choices. You'll learn how to eliminate mental noise, focus on what truly matters, and develop the kind of clear, decisive thinking that defines great leaders.

A step-by-step roadmap for rewiring your brain in 30 days

Rewiring your brain isn't about quick fixes or overnight transformations, it's about consistent, deliberate practice that builds new neural pathways. This 30-day plan breaks down the process into manageable steps, focusing on one core mental skill each week while building upon previous progress.

Week 1: Foundation Building (Days 1-7) The first week focuses on creating mental space and establishing baseline habits. Each morning, spend 10 minutes in focused observation—notice your thoughts without judgment. This practice strengthens your prefrontal cortex, the brain region responsible for executive function and decision-making.

- Days 1-2: Practice mindful observation for 10 minutes
- Days 3-4: Add pattern recognition exercises
- Days 5-7: Introduce basic problem-solving challenges

Week 2: Pattern Breaking (Days 8-14) Now we begin disrupting automatic thought patterns. Challenge yourself to take different routes to work, use your non-dominant hand for simple tasks, or solve problems backward. These exercises create new neural connections and enhance cognitive flexibility.

The brain resists change through a process called homeostasis—it prefers familiar patterns even when they don't serve us well. Breaking these patterns requires deliberate effort and consistency. Start small: change your morning routine, read different types of books, or engage with people outside your usual circle.

Week 3: Mental Agility Training (Days 15-21) This week introduces more complex cognitive challenges.

Each day, tackle one difficult problem before noon when your prefrontal cortex is most active—practice switching between different types of thinking—analytical, creative, and strategic.

Remember Sarah, the software developer who struggled with rigid thinking patterns. She started small, spending five minutes each morning solving puzzles that required different thinking styles. Within weeks, she noticed improvements in her problem-solving abilities at work and better adaptability to unexpected challenges.

Week 4: Integration and Application (Days 22-30) The final phase combines everything you've learned into practical applications. Create scenarios that require quick thinking, emotional regulation, and adaptive problem-solving. Practice making decisions under time constraints while maintaining mental clarity.

- Days 22-25: Combine multiple cognitive skills in real-world scenarios
- Days 26-28: Practice rapid decision-making exercises
- Days 29-30: Review and reinforce new mental habits

Throughout this process, track your progress in a mental agility journal. Note specific improvements in your thinking patterns, decision-making speed, and problem-solving abilities. This isn't just about completing exercises, it's about building lasting neural pathways that support clearer, faster, and more adaptable thinking.

The key to success lies in consistency rather than intensity. Small, daily actions create more lasting change than sporadic bursts of effort. Your brain forms new neural connections through repetition and focused attention, not through occasional intense sessions.

Think of this process like learning a new language—you wouldn't expect to achieve fluency after just one intensive day of study. Instead, regular practice, even in short bursts, creates lasting neural pathways that become automatic over time.

Each week builds upon the previous one, creating a compound effect that transforms how your brain processes information and responds to challenges. By day 30, you'll notice improved mental clarity, faster decision-making, and greater adaptability to change.

Remember, this isn't about becoming a different person; it's about optimizing your brain's natural capacity for growth and adaptation. The goal is to think more clearly, make more informed decisions, and adapt more readily to whatever challenges come your way.

Daily and weekly challenges to build a sharper, faster, and more adaptable mind

Building a sharper mind isn't about sporadic bursts of effort; it's about consistent, deliberate practice through specific daily and weekly challenges that target different aspects of cognitive function. Let's break down these challenges into practical exercises you can implement immediately.

Daily Morning Challenges (15-20 minutes):

- Solve one complex problem before checking your phone
- Read material outside your expertise for 10 minutes
- Write down three different solutions to a current challenge
- Practice focused observation of your environment for 5 minutes

These morning exercises prime your brain for clearer thinking throughout the day. Within weeks, you'll notice improved problem-solving abilities during morning meetings and better mental clarity throughout the day.

Weekly Deep-Dive Challenges:

- Monday: Memory Enhancement - Learn one new skill or concept
- Tuesday: Pattern Recognition - Study systems in different fields
- Wednesday: Decision-Making - Practice rapid analysis of complex situations
- Thursday: Perspective Shifting - Examine problems from multiple angles
- Friday: Creative Problem-Solving - Generate multiple solutions
- Weekend: Integration and Reflection

Imagine stepping outside your usual routine, much like taking on a new creative challenge each week. At first, it might feel uncomfortable to explore areas beyond your expertise—maybe it's studying art composition on Thursdays or trying a completely different hobby. However, as you persist, you'll begin to notice fresh insights and more innovative solutions in your daily work.

These new perspectives can completely transform how you approach problems and spark unexpected breakthroughs.

Monthly Growth Challenges:

- Week 1: Focus on speed of analysis and decision-making
- Week 2: Develop cognitive flexibility through varied tasks
- Week 3: Build pattern recognition across different domains
- Week 4: Integrate and apply new thinking methods

The key to these challenges lies in their progressive nature. Start with manageable tasks and gradually increase complexity. For instance, begin with simple pattern recognition exercises, such as identifying sequences in numbers, and then progress to recognizing patterns in market trends or human behavior.

Track your progress using specific metrics:

- Decision-making speed in familiar situations
- Ability to switch between different types of thinking
- Number of alternative solutions generated for problems
- Speed of pattern recognition in new situations

Remember that mental agility isn't about constant intensity, it's about consistent practice and gradual improvement. Just as athletes don't train at maximum intensity every day, your brain needs a balance of challenge and recovery.

Incorporate these challenges into your existing routine rather than treating them as separate tasks. During your commute, practice observation skills. While reading the news, identify patterns across different stories. Turn everyday situations into opportunities for mental training.

A crucial aspect often overlooked is the power of varied exposure. Engage with different types of thinking:

- Analytical (through logic puzzles and problem-solving)
- Creative (through imagination exercises and innovation challenges)
- Strategic (through scenario planning and decision trees)
- Intuitive (through pattern recognition and gut-feeling awareness)

The brain strengthens through challenge, adapts through variety, and grows through consistent practice. These exercises aren't just about getting smarter; they're about building a more adaptable, resilient mind capable of navigating an increasingly complex world.

Create accountability by sharing your challenges with others or joining a group focused on mental agility. This social element adds motivation and provides different perspectives on problem-solving approaches.

Remember to adjust these challenges based on your progress and needs. If specific exercises become too easy, increase their complexity. If others prove too difficult, break them down into smaller steps. The goal is steady progress, not perfection.

Through consistent practice of these challenges, you'll develop not just sharper thinking, but a more adaptable mind capable of handling whatever challenges come your way. This isn't about temporary improvement—it's about building lasting cognitive strength that serves you in every aspect of life.

Key takeaway: It's not about "knowing"—it's about consistent action

Knowledge without action is like having a high-performance car but never learning to drive. You can study every detail about the engine, memorize the manual, and understand the theory of acceleration—but until you get behind the wheel and practice, that knowledge remains potential energy, never converted into kinetic force.

Consider Sophie, a sharp and ambitious analyst who spent years collecting certifications and degrees. She could break down complex business strategies, recite management theories, and analyse market trends with flawless precision. But when it came time to make real decisions, she often froze, stuck between knowing what to do and taking action.

Her turning point came when she stopped chasing more credentials and started focusing on execution. Instead of signing up for yet another course, she set a simple goal: make one clear decision each morning before overthinking could take over. She started practicing fast decision-making on low-stakes tasks to build confidence. Within a few months, Sophie's ability to act decisively improved more than it had in years of studying theory.

Top performers aren't necessarily those who know the most, they're the ones who consistently execute, learn from results, and adjust their approach. They understand that mental agility isn't about storing information, it's about developing the neural pathways that connect knowledge to action.

The brain strengthens through use, not theory. Each time you make a decision, solve a problem, or adapt to a new situation, you're not just applying knowledge—you're building stronger neural connections. This process, called myelination, literally makes your brain's circuits more efficient through repeated use.

To build these pathways, focus on consistent practice rather than perfect execution:

- Start with small decisions to build confidence.
- Create daily opportunities to exercise judgment.
- Reflect on outcomes to refine your approach.
- Gradually increase the complexity of challenges.

Think of mental agility like physical fitness—reading about exercise won't make you stronger. You need consistent training, progressive challenges, and regular practice to develop real capability. The same applies to your mind.

Remember that consistency trumps intensity. It's better to make ten small decisions daily than to tackle one massive challenge weekly. Each action strengthens your mental pathways, making the next decision slightly easier.

Set up systems that ensure regular practice:

- Create daily decision points in your routine.
- Establish regular review periods to assess outcomes.
- Build feedback loops that inform future choices.
- Track your execution rate, not just your knowledge gains.

The goal isn't to eliminate uncertainty or guarantee perfect outcomes. Instead, focus on building the mental muscles that allow you to act decisively despite uncertainty. This comes through practice, not study.

Your brain rewires itself through consistent action. Each decision, each adaptation, and each problem solved creates stronger neural pathways. This is how knowledge transforms into capability—through regular, deliberate practice rather than passive understanding.

Start today. Choose one area where you've been hesitating, break it down into small decisions, and begin taking action. Remember: mental agility isn't about what you know—it's about what you do consistently with what you know.

The 30-day plan we've covered provides more than just a temporary boost in mental performance. It lays the foundation for a sustainable approach to cognitive development, one that acknowledges the brain's natural capacity for growth while respecting its need for structured, progressive challenges. By breaking down complex mental skills into manageable daily practices, we've seen how small, consistent actions create lasting neural pathways that support clearer thinking and faster decision-making.

But perhaps the most crucial lesson is this: mental agility isn't about accumulating knowledge—it's about developing the capacity to act decisively in moments that matter.

Remember that your mind, like any complex system, responds to regular training and deliberate practice. The exercises and challenges outlined here aren't meant to be completed and forgotten—they're tools for ongoing development, adaptable to new challenges and changing circumstances.

The journey of mental development is inherently unfinished, constantly evolving. Whether you're making business decisions, solving complex problems, or navigating personal challenges, the frameworks and practices in this chapter provide a foundation for clearer thinking and more confident action. The key isn't perfection but progress—measured not in knowledge gained, but in the consistent application of these principles in real-world situations.

CHAPTER 10

THE UNFINISHED MINDSET: HOW TO KEEP EVOLVING FOR LIFE

The greatest achievers don't succeed by staying the same—they evolve, adapt, and reinvent themselves to stay ahead. You'll discover how Michael Jordan transformed his game to dominate basketball, why embracing change is the key to lasting success, and how you can train your mind to continuously grow, pivot, and thrive in an ever-changing world. What truly sets champion athletes apart isn't just their physical prowess—it's their commitment to continuous evolution. Jordan's journey from an explosive scorer to a complete player exemplifies the power of an unfinished mindset. His story reveals a fundamental truth about success: those who reach the top don't stop growing once they get there.

In today's rapidly changing world, this lesson matters more than ever. Technologies evolve, industries transform, and skills that were valuable yesterday might become obsolete tomorrow. The most successful individuals and organizations share one critical trait: they treat their minds as works in progress, constantly adapting and refining their thinking to meet new challenges.

Michael Jordan wasn't just the most talented player in basketball—he was the most adaptable. Early in his career, he was known for his explosive athleticism, dominating the game with raw speed, power, and highlight-reel dunks. But when defenses figured out how to slow him down, he didn't resist change. He evolved. Jordan reinvented his game, mastering the mid-range fadeaway, improving his post moves, and transforming himself into an elite defender. When people doubted he could win championships, he adjusted his mindset, built mental toughness, and led the Chicago Bulls to six NBA titles. His ability to continuously learn, adapt, and refine his skills made him unstoppable.

But Jordan's greatest test came after he retired from basketball for the first time. Instead of staying in his comfort zone, he challenged himself to start from scratch in a completely different sport—professional baseball. Though he struggled, the experience forced him to relearn discipline, humility, and patience. When he returned to the NBA, he was mentally sharper, strategically smarter, and more determined than ever. His second act with the Bulls cemented his legacy—not just as a great player, but as someone who never stopped evolving. Jordan's story is proof that true success isn't about talent alone—it's about constantly reinventing yourself to stay ahead of the game.

Today, we'll explore how to cultivate this unfinished mindset—the mental framework that enables you to stay curious, embrace change, and continue growing, regardless of how much you've already achieved. You'll learn practical strategies for continuous learning, techniques for maintaining mental flexibility, and methods for turning uncertainty into opportunities. Because in a world that never stops changing, the most valuable skill isn't what you know now—it's your ability to keep evolving for life.

Your biggest enemy? Comfort and certainty

Comfort is a silent killer of potential. It wraps around you like a warm blanket, whispering that you're safe, that you've learned enough, that you can finally relax. But in today's world, comfort is a dangerous illusion.

You might have spent years mastering a skill, knowing every detail, every shortcut, and feeling confident that your expertise makes you indispensable. But when new technologies or approaches emerge, you face a choice: step out of your comfort zone to learn and grow or cling to what you already know and hope it will be enough.

If you choose comfort, you risk becoming outdated faster than you think. Sticking to old knowledge might feel safe in the moment, but it can leave you struggling to stay relevant while others move ahead. Embracing change and continuously learning is what keeps you competitive and future-ready.

The human brain is wired to seek certainty and avoid discomfort. This evolutionary trait helped our ancestors survive by sticking to what was safe and known. But in today's rapidly evolving world, this same instinct can become our greatest liability. The more comfortable you are, the more resistant you become to change, and the harder it becomes to adapt when change inevitably arrives.

This is why many successful organizations deliberately create discomfort. They rotate employees through different roles, challenge established processes, and encourage experimentation. They understand that comfort breeds complacency, while controlled discomfort drives growth.

The antidote to comfort isn't chaos—it's calculated risk-taking. It's deliberately putting yourself in situations where you don't have all the answers. It's choosing to learn a new skill before you need it. It's questioning your assumptions even when they've served you well.

Here's a practical way to break free from the comfort trap: Every month, identify one area where you feel too comfortable. It could be your morning routine, your problem-solving approach, or your professional skills. Then, introduce a deliberate disruption. Take a different route to work. Solve problems using unfamiliar methods. Learn a skill that seems irrelevant to your current needs.

The goal isn't to make yourself perpetually uncomfortable. Instead, it's to develop what psychologists call 'comfort with discomfort'—the ability to stay calm and focused when facing uncertainty. This mental flexibility becomes increasingly valuable as the pace of change accelerates.

Remember: The most dangerous comfort zone isn't physical—it's mental. It's the belief that what you know today will be enough tomorrow. It's the assumption that your current thinking patterns will serve you indefinitely. In a world where industries can transform overnight, this mental rigidity isn't just limiting—it's potentially catastrophic.

The paradox of growth is that it requires us to embrace uncertainty. Every significant breakthrough in history has come from someone willing to question certainty, to step beyond comfort, and to explore the unknown. Your mind is no different. It grows strongest when challenged, when pushed beyond familiar territory, when forced to adapt to new realities.

So, ask yourself: Where have you become too comfortable? What assumptions about your work, your skills, or your thinking patterns have remained unchallenged? These questions aren't meant to create anxiety about the future—they're invitations to grow before growth becomes necessary.

The one rule for lifelong mental growth: Stay curious

In 1968, a young researcher named George Land conducted a groundbreaking study on creativity in children. He tested 1,600 five-year-olds using the same creativity test NASA used to select innovative engineers and scientists. The results were stunning: 98% of five-year-olds scored at the 'genius' level for divergent thinking. When he retested the same children at age 10, only 30% scored at this level. By age 15, the number dropped to 12%. When he tested adults, the number fell to a mere 2%.

This study revealed a sobering truth: we don't lose our ability to think creatively—we unlearn it. We trade curiosity for conformity, wonder for certainty, and questions for answers. But the most successful individuals and organizations do the opposite; they cultivate curiosity as their primary competitive advantage.

Imagine being a teacher and watching your students struggle with a subject you know they can master. Instead of sticking to the same old methods, what if you asked yourself: *"How could this be taught differently?"* Maybe you explore storytelling, games, or real-life applications. Suddenly, engagement skyrockets, understanding deepens, and what once felt impossible starts to fall into place.

Success doesn't come from having all the answers — it comes from asking better questions. Curiosity isn't just about questioning; it's about staying actively interested in how things work, why they work that way, and exploring new possibilities. It means approaching the familiar with fresh eyes and seeing obstacles as puzzles waiting to be solved, not walls to avoid. That's how real breakthroughs happen.

Here are three practical ways to cultivate lifelong curiosity:

- Question Your Defaults: Every day, identify one thing you do automatically and ask why you do it that way. This simple practice prevents mental autopilot and keeps your thinking fresh.
- Cross-Pollinate Your Interests: Read books outside your field. Study how other industries solve problems. Some of the most innovative solutions come from applying ideas across different domains.
- Embrace the Amateur's Mind: When you're an expert, it's easy to stop noticing details. Regularly put yourself in learning situations where you're a beginner.

The power of curiosity extends beyond personal growth—it's becoming increasingly valuable in the professional world. A 2018 workplace study found that organizations that cultivate curiosity report higher levels of innovation, reduced group conflict, and more adaptable responses to market changes.

Curiosity also serves as a natural antidote to fear and uncertainty. When you're genuinely curious about a challenge, you focus less on what might go wrong and more on what you might discover. This shift in perspective transforms threatening situations into learning opportunities.

The key is maintaining curiosity even when—especially when—you think you already know the answer. Every assumption is an opportunity for discovery. Every certainty is a chance to learn something new. Every expertise is a platform for further exploration.

Remember: Curiosity isn't just a trait—it's a practice. It requires regular exercise, deliberate cultivation, and sometimes, the courage to question what everyone else takes for granted. In a world where knowledge doubles every few years, the ability to stay curious isn't just helpful, it's essential for survival and success.

Your mind is a garden, and curiosity is the water that helps it grow. Without regular cultivation, even the most fertile ideas can wither. However, with consistent nurturing, your mental landscape can continue to expand, evolve, and produce fresh insights throughout your entire life.

Final exercise: Design your mental agility blueprint for life

Throughout this book, we've explored the principles, strategies, and habits that build mental agility. Now, it's time to create your personalized blueprint—a concrete plan for ongoing mental evolution that aligns with your unique goals and challenges.

Your mental agility blueprint isn't a rigid set of rules. Instead, think of it as a living document that grows with you, adapting as you face new challenges and opportunities. Let's break this exercise into actionable steps that will help you design your path forward.

Step 1: Assess Your Current Mental LandscapeTake out a notebook and evaluate your thinking patterns across these key dimensions:

- Decision-Making Speed: How quickly do you process information and reach conclusions?
- Adaptability: How do you respond when plans change unexpectedly?

- Problem-Solving: What's your typical approach when facing obstacles?
- Learning Agility: How readily do you acquire and apply new skills?
- Emotional Regulation: How well do you maintain clear thinking under pressure?

Rate yourself from 1-5 in each area, with specific examples of when you've demonstrated strength or struggled in these dimensions.

Step 2: Define Your Growth ZonesIdentify three specific areas where improving your mental agility would create the most significant impact in your life. These might include:

- Professional advancement opportunities
- Personal relationship dynamics
- Creative projects or innovations
- Leadership responsibilities
- Life transitions or challenges

For each area, write down what improved mental agility would look like in practice.

Step 3: Design Your Daily PracticeCreate a personalized schedule for mental training that suits your lifestyle. Start small but remain consistent. Here's a framework to build upon:

Morning Routine (15 minutes):

- Read material that challenges your assumptions.

- Practice decision-making exercises.

- Review and adjust daily goals.

Midday Check-in (5 minutes):

- Assess emotional state and thinking clarity.

- Adjust approach based on morning experiences.

- Reset focus if needed.

Evening Review (10 minutes):

- Document key decisions and their outcomes.
- Identify learning moments from the day.
- Plan tomorrow's mental challenges.

Step 4: Build Your Support System Mental agility thrives in the right environment and with the proper support. Create your ecosystem:

- Find a thinking partner who challenges your perspectives.
- Join or create a group focused on continuous learning.
- Set up regular review sessions to track your progress.
- Identify resources and tools that enhance your practice.

Step 5: Create Your Feedback Loop Establish metrics to track your mental agility development:

- Keep a decision journal documenting key choices and outcomes.
- Set monthly review dates to assess progress.
- Gather feedback from colleagues and mentors.
- Measure improvements in specific challenge areas.

Step 6: Plan for Obstacles Anticipate what might derail your mental training and prepare contingency plans:

- Time constraints: Break training into smaller, manageable segments.
- Energy dips: Align challenging tasks with your peak mental hours.

- Resistance to change: Create accountability partnerships.
- Setbacks: Develop specific recovery protocols.

Remember, this blueprint is about progress. Start with what feels manageable and adjust as you grow. The goal is to develop sustainable habits that enhance your cognitive abilities over time.

Implementation Tips:

- Start with one focus area and master it before adding more
- Schedule weekly reviews to refine your approach
- Document breakthroughs and challenges
- Adjust your blueprint quarterly based on results
- Share your progress with others to stay accountable

Your mental agility blueprint should evolve as you do. Review and revise it regularly, celebrating progress while identifying new areas for growth. This isn't just a one-time exercise, it's your framework for lifelong mental development.

Take action now: Grab a notebook and begin with Step 1. The sooner you start mapping your mental evolution, the sooner you'll see results. Remember, mental agility is about reaching a destination and about embracing the journey of continuous growth and adaptation.

This blueprint is your commitment to keeping your mind sharp, adaptable, and ready for whatever challenges lie ahead. By following these steps and maintaining consistent practice, you're preparing for the future and actively shaping it through enhanced mental capabilities.

This book began with a simple truth: your mind is never finished. We explored how rigid thinking led to Kodak's downfall, how mental traps keep us stuck in outdated patterns, and how the ability to adapt separates those who thrive from those who merely survive. Now, as we conclude, it's clear that mental agility isn't just another skill, it's the foundation for all other skills.

Through stories of transformation, from Michael Jordan's evolution in basketball to Maria's innovative approach to teaching mathematics, we've seen how an unfinished mindset creates extraordinary results. These weren't just tales of success—they were demonstrations of what happens when someone refuses to let their thinking calcify.

The neuroscience is clear: our brains remain plastic throughout our lives, capable of forming new neural pathways and adapting to new challenges well into old age. This biological fact underscores the central message of this book—that mental growth isn't limited by age, experience, or current capabilities. It's limited only by our willingness to keep learning, to stay curious, and to embrace the discomfort that comes with new challenges.

But knowledge without action remains purely academic. That's why we've provided practical frameworks throughout this journey—from the 3-Second Rule for decision-making to the Mental Agility Blueprint for continuous growth. These aren't just theoretical concepts; they're battle-tested tools for navigating an increasingly complex world.

As you close this book, remember that the most valuable skill isn't what you've learned in these pages—it's your newfound ability to keep learning, adapting, and evolving. The mental frameworks, decision-making tools, and agility practices you've acquired are not destinations but launching points for continued growth.

In a world where artificial intelligence is reshaping industries, market dynamics shift overnight, and yesterday's solutions may become tomorrow's problems, mental agility isn't optional; it's essential. But unlike technological skills that can become obsolete, the ability to think clearly, adapt quickly, and make smart decisions under pressure only grows stronger with practice.

Your mind is indeed unfinished—and that's its greatest strength. Every challenge becomes an opportunity to grow stronger. Every setback becomes a chance to think differently. Every change becomes a catalyst for evolution.

The future belongs to those who maintain their curiosity, who challenge their assumptions, and who view their minds not as finished products but as works in progress. You now have the tools to be one of those people.

The real work begins here.

CONCLUSION

In 2007, a small team at Apple was racing to finish the first iPhone. The pressure was intense, deadlines were tight, and failure wasn't an option. Steve Jobs had promised the world a revolutionary device, but with just weeks before launch, the software kept crashing. The team was exhausted, stressed, and starting to doubt whether they could meet their delivery deadline.

Then, in a crucial meeting, Jobs shared a perspective that changed everything:

'Your minds are like parachutes—they only work when they're open."

He wasn't just talking about solving the immediate technical challenges. He was teaching them a fundamental truth about success in an ever-changing world: The ability to think clearly, adapt quickly, and stay mentally agile isn't just helpful—it's essential.

Throughout this book, we've explored how mental agility separates those who thrive from those who merely survive. We've seen how companies like Kodak fell because they couldn't adapt their thinking, while others, like Amazon, conquered new territories by remaining mentally flexible. We've learned that success isn't about having all the answers but about training your mind to find solutions no matter what challenges arise.

The world isn't slowing down. Technology will continue to evolve, industries will continue to transform, and the way we work and live will never stop changing. However, here's what won't change: The advantage will always go to those who can think clearly under pressure, adapt more quickly than their competitors, and identify opportunities where others see obstacles.

Your mind truly is unfinished—and that's its greatest strength. Like a master craftsman's tools, it must be continuously sharpened, refined, and upgraded. The mental strategies, frameworks, and exercises in this book aren't just theories, they're proven tools used by leaders, innovators, and achievers across every field.

Remember: The most intelligent people aren't those who know everything—they're the ones who can learn anything. Your greatest asset isn't your current knowledge, it's your ability to think, adapt quickly, and make wise decisions when it matters most.

As you close this book, remember that this isn't the end of your journey, it's just the beginning. Your mind is a powerful tool that grows sharper with every challenge you face, every perspective you consider, and every time you push beyond your comfort zone.

The future belongs to the mentally agile. Not because they're more intelligent or more talented than everyone else, but because they understand a simple truth: In a world that never stops changing, the ultimate competitive advantage is an unfinished mind—always learning, constantly adapting, always evolving.

Now it's your turn. Take these tools, practice these strategies, and train your mind to think clearer, work smarter, and adapt faster than ever before. Ultimately, success isn't just about where you are today; it's about how quickly you can evolve to meet the challenges of tomorrow.

Your mindset is the blueprint of your destiny—design it with vision, strengthen it with resilience, and success will become your way of life.

Your mind is your greatest asset. Keep it sharp. Keep it agile. And most importantly, keep it unfinished.

BIBLIOGRAPHY

Bezos, J. (2021). Invent and Wander: The Collected Writings of Jeff Bezos. Harvard Business Review Press.

Duckworth, A. (2016). Grit: The Power of Passion and Perseverance. Scribner.

Dweck, C. S. (2006). Mindset: The New Psychology of Success. Random House.

Ericsson, A., & Pool, R. (2016). Peak: Secrets from the New Science of Expertise. Houghton Mifflin Harcourt.

Gladwell, M. (2008). Outliers: The Story of Success. Little, Brown and Company.

Goleman, D. (1995). Emotional Intelligence: Why It Can Matter More Than IQ. Bantam Books.

Kahneman, D. (2011). Thinking, Fast and Slow. Farrar, Straus and Giroux.

LaFasto, F., & Larson, C. (2001). When Teams Work Best: 6,000 Team Members and Leaders Tell What It Takes to Succeed. SAGE Publications.

Merzenich, M. (2013). Soft-Wired: How the New Science of Brain Plasticity Can Change Your Life. Parnassus Publishing.

Oakley, B. (2014). A Mind for Numbers: How to Excel at Math and Science (Even If You Flunked Algebra). TarcherPerigee.

Sullenberger, C. (2009). Highest Duty: My Search for What Really Matters. William Morrow.

Taleb, N. N. (2012). Antifragile: Things That Gain from Disorder. Random House.

Willink, J., & Babin, L. (2015). Extreme Ownership: How U.S. Navy SEALs Lead and Win. St. Martin's Press.

www.ingramcontent.com/pod-product-compliance
Lightning Source LLC
Chambersburg PA
CBHW042029050526
44107CB00103B/770